RISE ABOVE CULTURE

ISAIAH 40:31

REV. J.C. BANDA

'Rise Above Culture' copyright © 2024

Rev. Josephat Chaponda Banda

The author has asserted his right to be identified as the author of this work in accordance with the Copyright, Designs and Patents Act 1988.

All rights reserved. No part of this publication may be reproduced, stored in a retrieval system, or transmitted, in any form or by any means, electronic, mechanical, photocopying, recording or otherwise without the prior permission of the author.

Scripture quotations are taken from the New International Version, NIV Study Bible and King James Version KJV

ISBN: 978-1-7385422-0-8

CONTENTS

Interpretations of Symbols and the Bible Text 5

Dedication 6

Acknowledgements 7

Introduction 8

CHAPTER 1 – Culture 10

    Why do people choose to do the wrong things instead of the right ones? 11

    Salvation from sin and eternal death 12

    Living above culture 13

CHAPTER 2 – Culture and its significance 16

    Biblical characters who rose above culture 19

    What is expected of people by God 20

CHAPTER 3 – The church as the salt and light of the world 23

    Church Outreach 24

CHAPTER 4 – God is at work lifting the weak and hopeless 32

    Practical Theology 36

CHAPTER 5 – People as stewards of themselves and other creatures 39

    Christian education 45

    Jesus and culture 46

Marriage 49
Family 51
Beware of social issues that destroy families 52
Third culture children and their future 54
Widows and widowers 56
Orphans in the society 56
God is at work with His people 58
Prayerful life as a necessity for the chosen ones 62
Giving hope to lone parents 69
With men this is impossible but with God all things
are possible (Matthew 19:26) 75
Hymns, gospel songs and choruses in the life of a
Christian believer 80
The significance of hymns and Christian songs 84
Important institutions for enlightenment 93
Social and economic stratification 103
Check your record 110
The decalogue as the will of God 112
Divine warning to mankind 114
Spiritual rebirth is a necessity 116
Be a good shepherd 118
Living in obedience to God 119
Take a stand in Jesus and you will not go wrong 120
Hunger and thirst after righteousness 121
God as the Sovereign Ruler 126
The role of the church is needed 129

References 132

INTERPRETATIONS OF SYMBOLS AND THE BIBLE TEXT

White – the sphere of enlightenment imbued with God's inspiration for the transformation of humanity and the environment.

Grey – the grey areas of any culture that needs enlightenment, for the transformation to please God our Creator and owner, for whom we were created.

The flying eagle – an enlightened individual inspired by God to do His will and discerns what is good or bad and right or wrong. One who "**Rises Above Culture**", through the inspiration of God the Sovereign Ruler of the universe and tries hard to live a righteous life, to please the omniscient and omnipresent God, in thought, word and deed.

Bible text, ISAIAH **40:31** – *"but those who hope in the Lord will renew their strength. They will soar on wings like eagles, they will run and not grow weary, they will not be faint."* NIV

"but they that wait upon the Lord shall renew their strength, they shall mount up with wings as eagles; they shall run, and not be weary; and they shall walk and not be faint." KJV

"To hope in the Lord is to plant the seed of faith and nourishing it."

It means praying as the Saviour did to God the Father.

"Yahweh, the Eternal God, shall strengthen all who Trust in Him."

DEDICATION

This book is in dedication to all the denominations that make up the church and whose primary duty is to preach the Gospel about Jesus Christ and teach the word of God to all the people in the world for their welfare and salvation from sin and eternal death. Failure to carry out Jesus' Great Commission, found in **Matthew 28:19–20**, is a serious negligence of duty and a detriment to the people whom God loves and would like to take into heaven indiscriminately provided they fear God, believe in His only begotten Son, our Lord and Saviour (**John 3:16**), according to the Christian belief. Gracious Lord, have mercy on us, as we seek to be righteous on earth. Our request to you is like that of Bartimaeus upon his encounter with Jesus, Son of David (**Mark 10:46–52**). We want to see what we cannot see for our welfare and salvation.

ACKNOWLEDGEMENTS

The author owes gratitude to the family members, Mrs. Mavis Banda (spouse), Mr M. Banda, Dr E. Banda, Mrs M. Nkomo, Mr R. Banda, Mr H.H. Banda, Mrs. D. Mawere, Mrs. T. Muganiwa, Mrs. T. Chiwara and Mr. S. Banda who created the conducive atmosphere for him to concentrate on writing the book, "Rise Above Culture." The discussions we had on the topic contributed to the writing of the book. Kuzivakwashe Chiwara – granddaughter, helped to type the manuscripts that have constituted this book for public consumption and for the family members whom the author is pastoring by sending motivational messages or lessons on spirituality and morality during his retirement as an ordained minister of the United Methodist Church in Zimbabwe. Working as busy as bees, has yielded this book which might be of assistance to the readers to be better stewards of God's people and other creatures, according to the will of God, the Holy One, basing on the Holy Bible, the canonised revelation of the salvific history which is the revelation of God to mankind.

INTRODUCTION

With passion, the author of this book "Rise above Culture" woke up early in the morning for some time to write down some ideas that got into his mind. For fear of forgetting these ideas, he thought it wise to capture, reflect and then share them with other people. The author believed that no matter how trivial these ideas might be, they could be sharpened or improved by people he shared them with in discussions. The author is in search of how to improve the morality of the people in the pluralistic society through Christian Ethics as a theological discipline that seeks to improve the morality of people in light of God or Jesus Christ, the incarnate Word and God's perfect revelation to mankind, for their salvation from sin and eternal death after the resurrection from the dead as Christians believe and recite in the Apostles' Creed.

People of ethnic groups, have different moral principles they have adopted to guide themselves in making decisions as to what is good or bad, right or wrong, just or unjust. The decisions they make, small or big, influence their actions which may be constructive or destructive, progressive or retrogressive. How, then can we lovingly and caringly live in peace with God by avoiding harming one another or each other in the society? Believers in one true God hold that God is the origin of all things on earth, living and non-living. All these things were created by God. Human beings are the image of God "imago Dei" and were given responsibilities over the other created things on earth, in other words, they are stewards who should act responsibly towards themselves and the other creatures in obedience to God their Creator and Owner. Doing good of any kind to fellow people and the environment, should be their obligation on earth. Any sinful or bad act to anyone is against the will of God hence in the Decalogue, found in Exodus 20:2–12, we read about the relationship required by God among the people. From verses 12 to 16 we read thus, "Honour your father and your mother so that you may live long in the land the Lord your God is giving to you.

[13] "you shall not murder."

[14] "you shall not commit adultery."

[15] "you shall not steal."

[16] "you shall not give false testimony against your neighbour."

[17] "you shall not covet your neighbour's house. You shall not covet your neighbour's wife or his male or female servant, his ox or donkey, or anything that belongs to your neighbour." (NIV study Bible)

These six commandments are to be followed in the society for the welfare of the people irrespective of colour, tribe or creed. Mutual respect and respect for life are to be observed in the world. People of all races enjoy peace and safety where such commandments are followed and the law enforcement agents will have their hard work alleviated. Who does not like to live in peace and safety? Who can choose to be disrespected, humiliated or treated unfairly? God is holy, omniscient and just; hence He wants people to live according to His will for them to have a foretaste of heavenly life where there is no tempter and sin. It is irrefutable that no one is perfect spiritually and morally but with self-control or discipline we can be better people in thought, word and deed. Theocentric and Christocentric instructions help people to transform their attitudes and behaviour for their mutual good as human beings created in the image of God. Everyday people make decisions small or big, bad or good. Therefore, they need guiding principles to behave responsibly for the good of all the people. A person living in the society, is a social being who should observe the social norms and values to live well with others and to please the Holy God and the Sovereign Ruler of the universe.

Chapter 1

CULTURE

It is something good and enlightening to understand what culture is and its significance in any society. The Oxford Compact English Dictionary Second edition, revised, explains culture as:

1. The arts and other manifestations of human intellectual achievement regarded collectively.

2. A refined understanding of appreciation of this.

3. The customs, institutions and achievements of a particular nation, people, or group".

In a culture, social beliefs, activities and formalised customs, are upheld with their norms and values observed, forming a cradle for social growth and the way of living of people. Violation of social norms and values, renders the perpetrators social misfits and a threat to the cohesion of the society for their welfare, development and prosperity. To dispel misguided attitudes and behaviour in the society, some kind of socialisation like teaching social etiquette and discipline should be enforced to improve the environment. Adults should demonstrate good morals to set good examples to the children they nurture to adulthood. Children are to be reminded of good conduct at home, school, and church so that they adhere to practices that can lead them to be people of integrity even at their places of employment when they are adults.

As children grow up, they are spiritually and morally vulnerable just as they are physically. They need to be protected and guided to be morally good rather than to be left alone to discover what is good or bad, right or wrong and why. When children are not carefully monitored in behaviour, they will be more vulnerable to evil forces around them to the extent of becoming uncontrollable in behaviour. They will be lured into peer groups and disrupt their precious time of learning to prepare themselves for a bright future for employment. Bad habits in the developmental stages of the children should be nipped in the bud.

Why do people choose to do the wrong things instead of the right ones?

'The cause and effects' principle in life is natural. If bad habits are often practised, they end up being part of one's character and so are the good practices. Theologians talk about the original sin which is said to be inherent in the human beings. This begins with the fall of the first man, Adam in the Garden of Eden (**GENESIS 3:1–24**). Adam disobeyed God and by so doing, he sinned. Sin resulted in death which is an irreversible natural phenomenon to all the descendants of human beings. In human beings, there is a tendency that is inclined to vice which is hereditary. The original man was sinless for God is holy and there was no tempter to mislead this man. In creating the first man in a special way according to the Holy Bible, it is stated: *"Then the Lord God formed a man from the dust of the ground and breathed into his nostrils the breath of life, and the man became a living being"* (**GENESIS 2:7**). This human being is in the group of animals which is classified as, "Homo sapiens" in original Latin which means 'wise man' as God breathed into him His breath of life. Therefore, a man is made up of body or flesh and soul – the outer person and the inner person that includes the spirit of life. When a person dies the inner person departs from the body and the body is buried into the ground from which it was formed by God originally. In the letter of Paul to the **ROMANS 5:12**, we read thus: *"Therefore just as sin entered the world through one man, and death through sin, and in this way, death came to all people, because they all sinned."* Because God breathed into a man His breath, there is something holy in him. He has conscience that can show him that there is God who should be obeyed and worshipped but the choice is his to worship or not, to choose what is right or wrong, bad or good. His judgement by God, His maker, is based on his choice. At times, a person acts in ignorance but according to the natural principle of living the "cause and effects" will take its course to the logical goal as it is stated in **Romans 6:23** *"For the wages of sin is death, but the gift of God is eternal life in Christ Jesus, our Lord."* Sin is a rebellion against God which a person cannot win because God is invincible or undefeated, "Deus Semper Invictus Est." Sin has some repercussions that can be experienced here on earth and hereafter, after the resurrection from death. In the book of **Daniel 12:2–3**, it is said: *"Multitudes who sleep in the dust of the earth will awake:some to everlasting life, others to shame and everlasting contempt. Those who are wise will shine like the brightness of the heavens, and those who lead many to righteousness, like the stars for ever and ever."* The Gospel according to **John 5:28–29**, expresses the concept of death and life after death when people resurrect thus: *"Do not be amazed at this, for a time is coming when all who are in their graves will hear his voice and come out– those who have done what is good will rise to live, and those who have done what is evil will rise to be condemned."*

Salvation from Sin and Eternal Death

To avoid the devastating death mentioned in the Holy Bible, the inspired word of God, people are urged to confess their sins to the omniscient and omnipresent God, ask for the forgiveness of their sins wholeheartedly and they will truly be forgiven to start writing their life stories on a clean page for God will have completely forgiven them. People should always run away from sin and the anger of God by living a clean life of righteousness the best way they can. When they believe in the Triune God, they spiritually live as safe living people and when they are dead, will be as safe dead people with hope to resurrect to live with God forever. This theological understanding is based on **John 3:16** *"For God so loved the world that he gave his one and only Son, that whoever believes in Him shall not perish but have eternal life."*

Repentance is to be done during the period of grace (**Luke 11:18–19**) when the body and the soul are still together on earth. There is no repentance after death. Let's learn from the Gospel according to Luke 16:19–31 where Jesus' parable of the "Richman and Lazarus" is vividly expressed for people to learn from it and prepare for their end of life on earth and new life hereafter in heaven. Spiritual things are based on reason and choice but not on coercion. An option of persuasion in the evangelisation of people is the way to follow in the making of disciples of Jesus Christ who has already won victory for all the people on earth. All that the people have to do is to accept Jesus as their personal Saviour according to the Christian 'Doctrine of Soteriology.'

Living Above Culture

To live above culture, takes human effort to surrender themselves to God their Maker as is sung by believers of God in the hymn: "Have Thine Own Way, Lord." Experiential theology is expressed by the believers here who seek God's wisdom in making decisions, that is, what is right or wrong, good or bad, just or unjust in light of the Holy God who is omniscient and just.

Have Thine Own Way, Lord

[1] Have Thine own way Lord
Have Thine own way
Thou art the potter I am the clay
Mould me and make me after Thy will
While I am waiting yielded and still

[2] Have Thine own way Lord
Have Thine own way
Search me and try me Master today
Whiter than snow Lord wash me just now
As in Thy presence humbly I bow

[3] Have Thine own way Lord
Have Thine own way
Hold over my being absolute sway
Filled with Thy spirit till all can see
Christ only always living in me.

The supernatural, immortal and Holy God, should make the inner and outer persons, His dwelling place, for an individual to have their mind to be like that of Jesus Christ as what Paul says in **Romans 12:2**: *"Do not conform to the patterns of this world, but be transformed by the renewing of your mind. Then you will be able to test and approve what God's will is – His good, pleasing and perfect will."* Like it is said, "The proof of pudding is in the eating." People should aspire to taste the heavenly food of the spirit or inner self. Nobody would like to mix good food with contaminated food which leads the inner self away from the will of God as people were created for God Himself, with responsibilities to God and the fellow people, to God's glory and people's joy. People should crave for the food of the Spirit for sound spirituality and morality to please God, our Maker like what Paul says in his letter to the **Galatians 5:22–26** which says, *"But the fruit of the Spirit is love, joy, peace, forbearance, kindness, goodness, faithfulness, gentleness, and self–control. Against such things there is no law. Those who belong to Christ Jesus have crucified the flesh with its passions and desires. Since we live by the Spirit, let us keep in step with the Spirit. Let us not become conceited, provoking and envying each other."*

Because of the original sin that is inherent in us human beings, the Christian virtue of self–control should be rife in us to curb the continuous inclination to vice. The fear of the Lord helps us to spiritually incline towards virtue for our salvation and establishment of good interactions with God and fellow people with whom we live to the joy and glory of God. Let's be advised by the word of God to enjoy the Kingdom of God on earth that will be consummated in heaven. The words of wisdom in the book of **Proverbs 1:17** say, *"The fear of the Lord is the beginning of knowledge, but fools despise wisdom and instruction."* **Proverbs 19:23** says, *"The fear of the Lord leads to life; then one rests content, untouched by trouble."*

Let's be aware of the fact that our theological reflection on ourselves is that the flesh is at war with the spirit in us which is an indication of the inherent original sin. In **Galatians 5:17**– Paul says, *"So I say, walk by the spirit and you will not gratify the desires of the flesh. For the flesh desires what is contrary to the Spirit and the Spirit what is contrary to the flesh. They* *conflict each other, so that you are not to do whatever you want. But if you are led by the Spirit, you are not under the law."* When the supernatural, which is spiritual and heavenly, enters the mundane or an earthly thing, which is mortal, a transforming miracle happens for a better living. God is love. He follows those who go astray to retrieve them from the spiritual and moral precipices where they can easily fall to death. God also follows those who fear Him to guide and protect them from the evil one whose aim is to tempt and trap the oblivious, unsuspicious and spiritually weak wanderers. "Vigilate et orate" watch and pray in this world and ask for a discerning spirit to differentiate good things from bad ones, what to do and what not to do in light of the Triune God.

Chapter 2

CULTURE AND ITS SIGNIFICANCE

Culture is made up of beliefs, customs, language, food, attire, utensils, and arts, like traditional dances and songs. Ethnic groups of people have different world views which make them do what they do for their existence on earth. These cultures have divine and human influences. Some practices are good and others in these cultures are not as they should be hence; they keep on changing in search of what is fitting for a better living. Culture is dynamic hence people experience new things in their way of living like types of food, dress, dances, language, clothes, dwelling places and modes of transport etc. Because of different norms and values that are adopted in these cultures, the saying "One man's meat is another man's poison" is irrefutable whereas polygamy and polyandry are acceptable in some cultures, in other cultures they are unacceptable. Whereas dog, crocodile, mice and snake meat is enjoyable in some cultures, they are taboos in other cultures.

Attitudes and practices should be viewed considering God or Jesus Christ. Anything that is not against the will of God is good and anything that pleases God though it displeases you personally is worthwhile to be accepted. Such an action is a sign of selflessness. Anything that is sinful in the sight of God is not to be tolerated because it is a snare of the devil.

The writer sees a culture metaphorically as a towel in which to wrap a baby for their warmth and comfort. The towel that has just been picked up should be examined to see whether it is devoid of certain elements on it that can cause discomfort to the baby who is to be diligently nurtured to the glory of our Maker. When people trust in God, they rise above culture and become theocentric and Christocentric in dealing with matters that need solutions with clear conscience. The most important thing is to please God for that which pleases God is good for people He created in His image whereas, what pleases people will not always be acceptable in the sight of God. Sometimes people agree to do something for bad intention to please themselves while fighting against the will of God, with ulterior motives. People at times, unite to act sinfully whereas God uses agape love and justice in dealing with issues for the people's common good. God is eternally immutable in His love and fulfilment of His promises to His people. He is faithful to Himself to remain Himself eternally. Human beings can be changeable hence sometimes they can easily break the promises they made to each other in marriages, families, churches, places of employment and in politics where promises are used for propaganda to attract voters who are always tantalised to get what they will never get as they are drawn to help the oppressors to remain in power for their own good. God wants the people to repent for the good of themselves and others who unnecessarily suffer in life.

As children of God by adoption, the Christians should set good examples of the citizens of the heavenly kingdom through their attitudes and behaviour for unbelievers to see the good deeds they do and praise God in heaven. The gospel according to **Matthew 5:16** says, *"in the same way, let your light shine before others that they may see your good deeds and glorify your Father in heaven."* If the church remains silent in the face of moral decadence in the society or in the world, how far different is the church from the salt that has lost its saltness? The church which is called 'Ekklesia' in Greek ('Ek' – out; 'Kaleo– I call) is made up of people called out of the world to serve God and the people. These people called out of the world are on God's mission and that mission is like Jesus' in the gospel according to **Luke 4:18–19** which reads thus: *"The Spirit of God is on me, because he has anointed me to proclaim good news to the poor. He has sent me to proclaim freedom for the prisoners and recovery of sight for the blind, to set the oppressed free, to proclaim the year of the Lord's favour."* Jesus whose body we are, as people born again of Spirit and water, are entrusted with high responsibilities. All Christian denominations put together, are called to be good and responsible for the souls of the people and their welfare spiritually, morally and socially. Heaven is big enough to accommodate all the people who were born in the past, who are born now and who will be born in future. The criteria for their chosenness are living a righteous life and to love God and fellow people as stated in the Gospel according to **Matthew 22:37–40**, Jesus replied the pharisees' question that was meant to test him by saying, *"Love the Lord your God with all your heart and with all your soul and with all your mind. This is the first and greatest commandment. And the second is like it; love your neighbour as yourself. All the law and the prophets hang on these two commandments."* Jesus summarised the Decalogue in **Exodus 20:1–17** into two commandments, The first four commandments of the Decalogue form the first commandment in Jesus' summary and the last six commandments form the second commandment. The Christian denominations that profess Jesus as the Lord and Saviour make up the church and have been given the responsibility by Jesus to preach and teach the word of God to mankind for their salvation.

After His resurrection and as He was preparing to ascend to heaven, the Lord Jesus Christ gave authority to the apostles to continue doing the work and He promised to be with them until the end of the known time. This is a high responsibility given to the church that should be carried out faithfully for the good of mankind. No angels from heaven will come down to tell people what they should do to qualify to enter heaven. The responsibility has been left in the hands of the church as an institution of salvation. People who are saved and accept Jesus as their personal saviour are empowered to do the work loyally. People of integrity will aim to do the Lord's work to please the one who sent them. There is a possibility of some Christians turning into pseudo-Christians by doing the work to enrich themselves and secularise the church which is meant to be sacred. In the sermon on the mount, Jesus taught about true and false disciples. He said that, *"not everyone who says to me, Lord, Lord; will enter the kingdom of heaven, but only the one who does the will of my Father who is in heaven.' Many will say to me on that day, 'Lord, did we not prophesy in your name and in your name drive out demons, and in your name perform many miracles? Then I will tell them plainly, I never knew you. Away from me, you evil–doers!"* **MATTHEW 7:21 –23**. Disciples of Jesus should learn the truth about the Triune God from the Holy Bible that teaches it faithfully and translate their faith into action to please Him.

The church is not to be commercialised to benefit those who want to be enriched by it materially but to be empowered spiritually, morally and economically to serve God, worship Him faithfully and obey Him. The church should be equipped by being taught and reminded what the Lord said and to help the needy (**MATTHEW 6:1–4**). The writer is impressed by the motto of Chisipiti High school in Harare, Zimbabwe written in Latin, 'Fons vitae Caritas' meaning the fountain or source of life is love or charity. There are many needy people who have been impoverished by social evil, ignorance, self–negligence, laziness and apathy. The church is called to teach and liberate people from such different types of bondages for them to see the meaning of life and its significance.

Biblical characters who rose above culture

In the story of the Deluge in **GENESIS 6:11–9:19**, Noah was chosen by God to perpetuate humanity after his wicked contemporaries had perished in the flood. In **GENESIS 6:8** we read thus, *"But Noah found favour in the eyes of the Lord."* To be called or chosen by God is to be elevated for service as a responsible person. In **ROMANS 8:30**, we read about the importance of being chosen and ordained to do the work of the Lord. Paul said, *"And those he predestined, he also called; those he called, he also justified; those he justified, he also glorified."*

God called Abraham to be an instrument of salvation in the entire world through himself and his descendants because of his obedience. Jesus was his descendent and became the expiation of the sins of the entire world.

Jacob the son of Isaac became the father of the twelve tribes of the Israelites because he feared God. One of his sons, Joseph, the dreamer, was guided, protected and he saved the chosen nation of Israel in Egypt to perpetuate the chosen nation in the fulfilment of God's plan to save people from sin and eternal death through the decalogue, the prophets and ultimately through Jesus, the Word incarnate, the only begotten Son of God.

King David, a man after God's own heart (**1 Samuel 13:14**), feared God and he became an ancestor of our Lord, Jesus Christ. When a person is chosen, they are there to fulfil God's plan for the salvation of mankind from different life bondages.

Moses was guided and protected from birth to the time he died in the desert as he was leading the liberated children of Israel to the Promised Land. He could communicate with God and the tablets with ten commandments as a covenant of Law, were given to him to announce to the children of Israel. He was a great leader in the liberation of the people of God from the Egyptian bondage in the salvific history of mankind.

Paul who was originally Saul, was dramatically called by Jesus to be an instrument of salvation through the propagation of the gospel. He became a missionary to the gentiles to fulfil Jesus' promise to the apostle in the book of **Acts 1:8** *"But you will receive power when the Holy Spirit comes in you, and you will be witnesses in Jerusalem and in all of Judea and Samaria and to the ends of the earth."*

What is expected of the people by God?

OBEDIENCE OR FAITH IN JESUS

Keeping God's commandments and internalising these commandments is to be part of us in thought, word and deed. That helps us to be consistent in doing things that please God. This is living righteously.

LOVE

God is love and the followers of Jesus, should love God by doing His will and worshipping Him. We should love our neighbours as we love ourselves. Baptism has a symbolical significance for people who are born again spiritually to become children of God born of God (**John 1:12–12; 3:3**). This baptism is a prerequisite for one to be adopted as a child of God and whose hallmark is love.

CONFESSION AND REPENTANCE

We should practise self-examination spiritually and morally to see if what we do complies with God's will. Whenever we find that we have gone astray, we should confess our sinful acts and ask God to forgive us – this is repentance. People learn from different racial groups and religious groups to improve their cultures through assimilation process as culture is dynamic.

PRESERVATION OF CULTURAL IDENTITY

People are who and what they are in their racial groups by God's choice as gifts of God to their parents. Babies are born and brought up in their cultural environment for socialisation and nurturing into adulthood. The races in which children are born in distinctive social or cultural mark of identity should be preserved in the pluralistic world for the divine purpose to be fulfilled through procreation. People should be proud of their identity and never worry about what they cannot change but what they can change. Inferiority and superiority complexes are to be avoided because they are against the will of God who created the people of different racial groups and God Himself was pleased with His creation.

One of the detrimental social practices is the discarding of one's language, for we use it for expressing ourselves meaningfully, the cultural activities and matters. A language is a means for social interaction in a cultural environment. You become richer in social interaction, if you learn more languages in addition to your own. It is wise to have culture centres for those of ethnic groups in the diaspora so that children can be taught to value their cultures. When they travel back to their original homes, they will not feel like a fish out of water when they communicate face to face with their relatives. Volunteers can help the children to master their languages in order to communicate eloquently with others.

Culture can be likened to a child in a portable bath tub. When the water in the bath tub is dirty, the mother does not pour away the dirty water together with the child but she carefully takes the child and keeps them safely out of the water then pours away the dirty water. This is what should be done in any culture. Any bad immoral practices should be uprooted for the welfare of the people in the society but the good ones ought to be kept and handed over to the next generation for their welfare and safety. Rising above culture is the social renaissance whereby the bad practices are replaced by the good ones for better living. It is the reawakening of the human mind.

Chapter 3

THE CHURCH AS THE SALT AND LIGHT OF THE WORLD

During His sermon on the Mount, Jesus referred to those who followed Him as the salt of the earth. During the time of Jesus, salt was a valued commodity. The followers of Jesus have a preserving influence. Salt was used to preserve meats and to slow decay. Christians should have preservative influence on their culture for the good of the earth which God loves. Christians, like salt to food, should add flavour in the society through their influence in better living where people love one another and treat each other as neighbours to be loved and cared for.

To be of value, Christians must keep their characteristics for which they ought to be known. As salt is known by its saltiness, the Christians should be known by love, the unconditional love which is the hallmark of a good Christian. When the Christians lose their flavour because they are corrupted by evil influences, they no longer serve the purpose for which they were called by Jesus. When Christians accommodate permissive living in their community, they behave as if they are blind. That is why it is said that there is no one more blind than a person who pretends to be blind. As one of a weak character, one is always in search of cheap popularity to be considered a good person by perpetrators of immoral acts. When a good person keeps quiet in the face of an evil, they are in support of the status quo. Paul in his second letter to Timothy says, *"All scripture is God breathed and is useful for teaching, rebuking, correcting and training in righteousness so that the servant of God may be thoroughly equipped for every good work"* **2 TIMOTHY 3:16–27**. It seems some human rights are prohibitive in correcting some activities in the society from the Christian point of view because Christianity is not the dominating institution of influence. If Paul's approach in **2 Timothy 3:16–17** is done within the church whose canon is the Holy Bible, his approach of correcting wrongs is acceptable and yet the world is supposed to be the church's parish. If the church remains quiet, sin will multiply to the detriment of the society.

Jesus, in His sermon on the mount, referred to His followers as the light of the earth – "Lucem terrae." They should function like the light in the world. They should be like a city on a high hill that cannot be hidden but let their light so shine before men, that they may see their good works and glorify their father in heaven (**Matthew 5:16**). Jesus gave the church a great responsibility of being the light in the world. This responsibility was originally solely the responsibility of Jesus who was the light in the darkness. "Lux in Tenebris." **John 1:5a**. The Christians are givers of the light. They should have great concern for other people as they have for themselves. They should play the role of guides in the society spiritually and morally. They are somehow either fulfilling or failing to fulfil that given responsibility. The light is needed because the world is in darkness and if Christianity imitates the darkness, it has nothing to show the world. To be effective, Christianity must display its distinctive characteristics of doing good works so that others will glorify God but not for self-glory. Christians must teach about God, His kingdom and people's response to God's revelation for them to be in harmony with God their Maker and the Sovereign Ruler of the whole universe. The Christians' divine vocation by the transcendent God is so great that it calls for faithfulness and devotion upon one who is called. God wants His word to reach every person for their salvation through faith and by God's grace at the end of the known time.

Church Outreach

When Jesus resurrected from the dead, He was given authority by God, His Father to extend to the whole world for God's rule to be experienced by people for their salvation. Jesus said to His disciples, *"All authority in heaven and earth has been given to me. Therefore, go and make disciples of all nations baptising them in the name of the Father and of the Son and of the*

Holy Spirit and teaching them to obey everything I have commanded you. And surely, I am with you always to the very end of the age" (**MATTHEW 28:18–20**).

To evangelise the unbelievers, calls for dedication and love for other people as we love ourselves. That spirit of selflessness to serve other people in various ways as teachers, doctors, scientists, farmers, nurses, ministers of religion to mention a few front-line workers, demands something more than self-economic desires. This is how God works invisibly in people in serving others.

An occasion once happened in the life of the writer, that a student at Nyamuzuwe High School in Zimbabwe – where he was a minister of religion and a school Headmaster – passed his form four examinations with flying colours but his father could not afford to send him to Fletcher High School where he had got a place to further his education in Form Five, The student approached his Headmaster and explained his plight, The Headmaster in turn, called for an urgent staff meeting in the school library to discuss the burning issue of the student by the name of Paidon Chiwaka of Kowo Village in Mutoko, Zimbabwe. After discussing the issue, we resolved to make some contributions to raise Paidon Chiwaka's first term's fees. Paidon was visibly shaken by excitement and thanked the teachers for the help given to him contrary to his expectation.

Paidon made his way to Fletcher High School in Gweru, Zimbabwe where he was enrolled for Form Five education. One day, a book seller by the name of Mr. Gumbanjera of Murewa District, Zimbabwe paid the Nyamuzuwe High School a visit with the intention of advertising the school text books. After discussing with him Paidon's situation, he decided to take over the responsibility of paying the school fees of Paidon for part of Form Five and the whole of Form Six education. The ambitious student of whom the Nyamuzuwe High School was very proud as its product, excelled in his studies and passed his Form Six Examinations with a high grade that enabled him to acquire a place at the Zimbabwe University, the biggest and renowned university in Zimbabwe where he was enrolled to study Mining Engineering which he completed very well.

Paidon was liberated mentally through education for his welfare and for the good of the nation as he served in mines. He was able to raise his family from the low social stratum to a higher one.

The writer regards what the Nyamuzuwe High School teachers did, as an example of "***Rising Above Culture.***" To use one's very valuable and scarce money to assist someone in need, is loving one's neighbour as one loves themselves which is one of Jesus' two commandments. The writer had a similar experience when he was a student at Hartzell High School and Teachers' Training school where he was given a school scholarship to further his studies and later served the church schools as a teacher, Headmaster and Minister of the United Methodist Church respectively, until his retirement in March, 2020. The writer is where he is now by God's assistance through the United Methodist Church and School Staff at Hartzell High School and Teachers College.

When one rises above culture, one tries to defeat selfishness, corruption and pride in order to uphold Jesus' principle of Agape Love – the unconditional love, the love that loves despite anything, the love that goes beyond boundaries to reach someone in need of help as what Jesus taught in His parable about "The Good Samaritan" in the Gospel according to **Luke 10:25–37**. Jesus, the greatest teacher on earth, one who is coeternal with God the Father and God the Holy Spirit, did what He did on earth in agreement with God the Father and revealed all what the Triune God wants us to obey and do to please Him and for people to be saved from sin and eternal death. Jesus came into the world to liberate us from different types of bondages and ushered into the world a period of grace when we can confess and repent from our sins to be forgiven by God. After death, there is no time for repentance and forgiveness from God. Jesus, the Son of God and the Saviour, will come as the Judge to judge the nations of the earth according to what they did on earth (**John 3:18**; **Romans 3:9–12**; **Acts 17:29–30**; **1 Peter 4:17**; **Romans 14:12**; **Ecclesiastes 12:14**; **2 Peter 2:9**; **James 2:13**; **2 Corinthians 5:10**; **1 John 4:17**.)

People should rise above culture during our period of grace when the body and the soul are still intact and our repentance and forgiveness from God are possible. Rising above culture should start from the inner person, the soul where attitudes are turned towards virtue rather than towards vice. Practising to do what is acceptable to God is to be liberated spiritually, mentally and physically. Inclination towards vice is a sin of living in bondage from which Jesus Christ came to liberate us among other types of bondages. When we hear the word of God, we should understand what it means to be transformed spiritually and morally. Sins are attractive but deadly and not worthy for our welfare as it is said, "It is not all gold that glitters." Not all attractive things are good to be taken for some of them are deadly.

To rise above culture is to fear God and love all people. The book of **Proverbs 9:10–12** says, *"The Fear of the Lord is the beginning of wisdom, and the knowledge of the Holy One is understanding. For through wisdom your days will be many, and years will be added to your life. If you are wise, your wisdom will reward you; if you are a mocker, you alone will suffer."* Theo-centric wisdom helps the believers to rise above culture in that it helps them to discern between right or wrong, good or bad, just or unjust before God who is omniscient and eternally righteous. King Solomon asked for this wisdom from God as he was a ruler of many people. He did not ask for wealth but wisdom rather than wealth, God gave him wisdom to rule with justice in the light of God and wealth (**1 Kings 3:1–5**). Ruling people in fairness is one of the characteristics of God, the Father who loves all people He created in His image – He calls a spade a spade in His holiness. Why should people refuse to take after Him who wants us all to live in peace and observe the rule of law? Rulers on earth are supposed to be the representatives of the invisible God who wants people to live righteously and justly wherever they are. God gave His message to the Israelites living in the Northern Kingdom through the Prophet Amos saying: *"I hate, I despise your religious festivals; your assemblies are a stench to me. Even though you bring me the burnt offerings and grain offerings, I will not accept them."* Though you bring choice fellowship offerings, I will have no regard for them. Away with the noise of your songs! I will not listen to the music of your harp. But let justice roll on like a river, righteousness like a never-failing stream!" **Amos 5:21–24**.

What is justice here? Did Jesus not teach about justice in His sermon on the mount? What did the Lord say to the people of the past and present? **Matthew 7:12** *"So in everything, do to others what you would have them do to you for this sums up the Law and the prophets."* In **Luke 4:18–19**, Jesus read from the book of **Isaiah 4:18–19** thus: *"The Spirit of the Lord is on me, because he has appointed me to proclaim good news to the poor. He has sent me to proclaim freedom for the prisoners and recovery of the sight of the blind, to set the oppressors free to proclaim the year of the Lord's favour."* Helping the people to be free from spiritual, physical and political bondages is implied in the word "Christos"– Christ which means liberator. God does not want people to be oppressed or ill-treated. When He says, "no more of this!" oppression comes to an end. God enthrones the earthly rulers in different ways for He is above them all. Those who disobey Him and rebel against Him will be defeated for God is invincible and immortal but earthly rulers are mortal and under God, the Sovereign Ruler who will judge all the earthly people; rulers, the rich and the poor, the powerful and the powerless. All that the people should do is to obey God and do good to all the people young or old, feeble or strong, educated or uneducated and the proud– they are all under Him, Paul says in his letter to the **Romans 14:11–13** *"It is written: 'As surely as I live, says the Lord,' every knee will bow before me; every tongue will acknowledge God." So then each of us will give an account of ourselves to God. Therefore, let us stop passing judgement in one another. Instead, make up your mind not to put any stumbling block or obstacle in the way of a brother or sister."* What God says seems very difficult for us on earth but when the Supernatural enters, the natural and the mortal a miracle takes place: As ordinary people we perform better in society in fear of the Lord. It is God who raises people to the level we never expected to reach to God's glory as expressed by Mary the mother of Jesus (Mater Dei) in her song, "The Magnificat" found in the Gospel of **Luke 1:52**," Deposuit potentes, de sede et exaltavit humiles." (Latin) *"He has brought down rulers from their thrones but has lifted up the humble."* The humble can be chosen and anointed to do wonderful work at the surprise of the powerful, the proud and self–seeking individuals for God to prove His power and fairness for He loves all people irrespective of their status in life. All people are the image of God. When God says, "Yes" nobody can say, "No." God is the ultimate Authority whether we doubt or do not believe it.

In obedience to the Lord's Great Commission, the United Methodist Church and other Church denominations have played very important roles in Africa and other continents in their Mission outreach where they have established churches in Zimbabwe and South Africa. Concentrating on the United Methodist Church, it has built sanctuaries, Mission Centres like Old Mutare Mission, Mutambara Mission in Manicaland Province in Mutare, Zimbabwe, Murewa Mission, Nyadire Mission, Nyamuzuwe Mission, Dindi Mission, Murehwa, Maramba Pfungwe District, Dendera Mission and the others in Mutoko District, Mashonaland East Province. The Church has built hospitals at Old Mutare Mission, Nyadire Mission and at Mutambara Mission and a clinic at Dindi Mission. It has built Orphanages at Old Mutare Mission and Nyadire Mission. It has a Teachers' Training College at Nyadire Mission. The United Methodist Conferences in Africa with the help of the United Methodist Church in the United States of America and Japan decided to establish Africa University at Old Mutare Mission, in Mutare, Zimbabwe which takes students from different parts of Africa like Zimbabwe, Republic of Congo, Angola, Mozambique, East Africa and South Africa. The university offers degrees to Ph.D. level.

The United Methodist Church together with the other denominations like Methodist Church in Zimbabwe, United Congregational Church in Zimbabwe, Anglican Church, Church of Christ and the Evangelical Lutheran Church contributed a lot to the establishment of the United Theological College in Hatfield, Harare, Zimbabwe where student pastors from these denominations study Diploma in Theology of the United Theological College and Diploma in Religious Studies offered by the University of Zimbabwe. The current Bishop E.K. Nhiwatiwa and his predecessor the late Bishop C. Jokomo first studied at this college before they went to the United States of America to further their studies. The writer went to the same college after the great and influential Bishops mentioned above.

After working as a teacher and the ordained minister of the United Methodist Church at Murehwa Mission and Murewa High School as an associate Pastor, School Chaplain, and teacher from 1978–1980, he was appointed in 1981 to go and reopen Nyamuzuwe High School that had been closed for three years during the Zimbabwe war of liberation. In 1989, he was appointed the District Superintendent of Murewa District. In 1990 he was appointed a lecturer and the Principal of the United Theological College from 1990–1996 at the college he was trained as a minister of religion.

In all the work that the church is doing, it is fulfilling what Jesus said in His Great Commission to His disciples and now the church is moving on with the Lord's words of encouragement, *"And surely I am with you always to the very end of the age"* **MATTHEW 28:20B**. These words of Jesus are very encouraging because we believe that God is immutable or unchangeable. What He promises, He fulfils to be faithful to Himself. It is Jesus who enables us to do His work as He taught us in **JOHN 15:5** "Ego eimi é ampelos umeis ta klemata." (Greek) – *"I am the Vine; you are the branches."* Our source of power is none other than Jesus whose body we are as Christians. Without Him we cannot achieve anything in His Vineyard. He enables us as His followers to keep on moving forward in faith in fulfilment of His plan as Paul says in **ROMANS 8:30**, *"And those He predestined, He also called, those He called, He also glorified."*

Individually or collectively let's rise above culture in assisting the needy, the desperate widows, orphans and in some cases, the needy elderly people or widowers as they need to be catered for, this takes sacrifice. Remember our Lord scarified His life to win victory for us by suffering on the cross for our sake. We are what we are as Christians, living in hope for eternal life hereafter because the Lord Jesus Christ "Agnus Dei"– the Lamb of God, died as an expiation for our sins to redeem us from sin and eternal death through faith in Him and by God's Grace. Let us rise above culture and inborn negative tendencies by applying love, kindness and self–control as Christian virtues in the society and fellow people will see the good deeds we do and praise God in heaven.

The United Methodist Church has now been granted a licence by the UK Government to operate in the UK as the Mission outreach of the Zimbabwe United Methodist Episcopal Area. There are now three ordained ministers in active ministry in the UK. The writer was serving in the UK since 2005 to the 31st March 2020. He also served as the District Superintendent from 2015–2018 covering the UK, Ireland and Australia– New Zealand.

The United Methodist Church, in the United Kingdom, started by shepherding the Zimbabweans in diaspora but now it is planning to serve people of other races also. The church has helped church members in different ways through the proclamation of the Word, visitations, counselling with encouragement and consolation in times of bereavement. Formation of teams for sports and recreation gave good time to the members in socialisation, to avoid moments of stress and isolation. During the time of Covid–19 lockdown, virtual church services and free conference calls have been held to pray and intercede for people in different situations in the world through prayers. Here, church members of different denominations gather and take turns to preach and sing hymns of different denominations. Encouraging testimonies are given on how the early morning proclamation of the word, prayers and testimonies have assisted them spiritually and mentally. These prayer meetings are held everyday form 5:00–7:00am. Bible study and discussions are held from 8:30–9:30 am. Such religious phenomena are in line with what Paul said in this first letter to the **THESSALONIANS 5:16– 22**.

"Rejoice always, pray continually, give thanks in all circumstances, for this is God's will for you in Christ Jesus. Do not quench the Spirit. Do not treat prophecies with contempt but test them; hold on to what is good, reject every kind of evil." Jesus earlier on said *"watch and pray so that you will not fall into temptation"* **MATTHEW 16:41A**. The Christians are urged to be spiritually alert and guard themselves against the tempter– "Vigilate et orate" – 'Watch and pray,' It is said joy or happiness is therapeutic for it repels stress and a feeling of loneliness.

Chapter 4

GOD IS AT WORK LIFTING THE WEAK AND HOPELESS

The God we worship is the God of history. He travels with us in the life journey to guide and protect us. What He wants from us is to be humble before Him so that we can be advisable. James, the brother of our Lord Jesus wrote in his letter that we must be humble before the Lord and He will lift us up (JAMES 4:10). To be humble is to be obedient and willing to learn from the Lord to rise above culture in our daily lives through His assistance.

 The Book of Discipline of the United Methodist Church, 2012 explains how God is at work in our lives to bring us salvation on earth through prevenient grace, justifying grace and sanctifying grace. We cannot save ourselves through deeds without faith, the gift of God to us. When we respond positively to God's revelation through Jesus, we understand God the Father well and we make up our minds to follow Him rather than not. If our response is negative, we resist the Spirit of God and choose not to obey Him. On grace, it is expressed this way: "Grace pervades our understanding of Christian faith and life. By grace we mean the undeserved, unmerited and loving action of God is undivided, it precedes salvation as "prevenient grace," continues in "justifying grace" is brought to fruition in "sanctifying grace."

In "prevenient Grace we acknowledge God's prevenient grace, the divine love that surrounds all humanity and precedes any and all of our conscious impulses."

In Justification and Assurance, "We believe God reaches out to the repentant believer in justifying grace with accepting and pardoning love:Wesleyan theology stresses that a decisive change in the human heart can and does occur under the prompting of grace and the guidance of the Holy Spirit. In justification we are, through faith, forgiven our sin and restored to God's favour."

The final stage of God's Grace to the repentant sinner is sanctification and perfection. If we cling to our faith in Jesus and try our best to live a righteous or clean life to the end of our life on earth, we are sanctified or cleansed to perfection to be acceptable in the sight of our Maker, to inherit the Kingdom of heaven. Though the grace of God surrounds all the people from birth to death, that cannot save us from sin and death. Our faith in God through Jesus complements God's grace for us to be saved as is said in **JOHN 3:16**, *"For God so loved the world that he gave his one and only Son, that whoever believes in him shall not perish but have eternal life."* Clinging to bad habits to please the body leads us to destruction for the earthly pleasures and wealth will end here on earth. Amassing wealth on earth illegally or immorally is a perilous exercise that leads to eternal death as it is told in Jesus' parable of the Rich fool in the Gospel according to **LUKE 12:13-21**. Spiritually and morally, bad practices before God, will not make us rise above culture but will lead us to our own doom on earth and in heaven. Rise above culture by abandoning evil practices so as to shine like a light on top of a hill.

Recurring social evils in the society are a great obstacle to people's rising above culture. The source of these evil practices is the inherited original sin of disobedience which begets insatiable desire for wealth, selfishness, envy and hatred. The devil is at the centre of all these practices to draw people to his side. The devil is now a wounded spiritual being through the death and resurrection of Jesus and powerless on believers in Jesus Christ. The devil does not own heaven and earth for they both belong to God (**DEUTERONOMY 10:14**; **PSALM 24**; **PSALM 95:4-5**).

There is a great need for self-control, the spirit of discernment and empathy in individuals in the society to curb the sufferings of the people, especially during this time of the natural disaster of Corona Virus disease, pandemic that has put the world into unbearable state of living. Some people need to have their hearts of stone removed to be replaced with hearts of flesh. Who can do that miraculous surgery but the heavenly Physician who moulded a human being? "Vigilate et orate!" Watch and pray! In **1 Peter 5:8–9**, Peter says: *"Be alert and of sober mind. Your enemy the devil prowls around like a roaring lion looking for someone to devour. Resist him, standing firm in the faith, because you know that the family of believers throughout the world is undergoing the same kind of sufferings."*

God affirms His presence among us through the incarnation of His only begotten Son on earth as stated in **Isaiah 7:17** and **Matthew 1:23**: *"The virgin will conceive and give birth to a son and they will call him Immanuel"* (which means "God with us"). God has many secret things that can be revealed to those who confide in Him as is hinted in **Jeremiah 33:3** *"Call to Me and I will answer you and will tell you great and unsearchable things you do not know."* To rise above culture people, need advice from God, who knows everything. In our social circumstances we should recite or sing the hymn titled: "***Guide me O My Great Redeemer***"

> [1] Guide me, O my great Redeemer,
> Pilgrim though this barren land,
> I am weak but you are mighty;
> Hold me with your powerful hand.
> Bread of heaven; bread of heaven,
> Feed me now and evermore,
> Feed me now and evermore.
>
> [2] Open now the crystal fountain,
> Where healing water flow
> Let the fire and cloudy pillar
> Lead me all my journey through
> Strong Deliverer, Strong Deliverer,
> Ever be my strength and shield,
> Ever be my strength and shield.
>
> [3] When I tread the verge of Jordan,
> Bid my anxious fears subside,
> Death of death, and hell's destruction,

Land me safe on Canaan's side,
Songs of praises, songs of praises
I will ever sing to you,
I will ever sing to you.

Another song to be sung for silent evangelism in the society where you may happen to be found, is: "**Let the Beauty of Jesus be seen in me.**"

[1] Let the beauty of Jesus be seen in me,
All His wonderful passion and purity,
Oh, Thou Spirit divine, all my nature refine,
Till the beauty of Jesus, be seen in me."

[2] When your burden is heavy
And hard to bear,
When your neighbours refuse all
Your load to share,
When you're feeling so blue,
Don't know just what to do,
Let the beauty of Jesus be seen in you.

[3] When somebody has been unkind to you,
Some word spoken that pierced you
through and through,
Think how He was beguiled, spat
upon and reviled,
Let the beauty of Jesus be seen in you.

[4] From the dawn of the morning
till close of day,
In example in deeds and in all you say,
Lay your gifts at His feet, ever
 strive to keep sweet,
Let the beauty of Jesus be seen in you.

Words By:Tom M. Jones
Music By:Albert W.T. Orsborn

Practical Theology

Texts to be read for the nourishment of the soul, to move on in faith are:
EPHESIANS 5:1-2 *"Be imitators of God, therefore as dearly loved children and live a life of love, just as Christ loved us and gave himself up for us as a fragrant offering and sacrifice to God". Matthew 5:16 "In the same way, let your light shine before men, that they may see your good deeds and praise your Father in heaven."*

PHILIPPIANS 3:20-21 *"But our citizenship is in heaven. And we eagerly await a Saviour from there, the Lord Jesus Christ, who by the power that enables him bring everything under his control, will transform our lowly bodies so that they will be like his glorious body."*

PHILIPPIANS 2:14-15 *"Do everything without grumbling or arguing, so that you may become blameless and pure, "Children of God without fault in a warped and crooked generation. Then you will shine among them like stars in the sky."*

MATTHEW 5:48 *"Be perfect, therefore, as your heavenly Father is perfect."*

1 JOHN 2:29 *"If you know that he is righteous, you know that everyone who does what is right has been born of him."*

The Holy Bible has many texts that will help those who want to rise above culture and shine like a house built on top of a hill. The Lord's Sermon on the Mount, Matthew 5,6,7, is full of teachings on spirituality and morality for the citizens of the Kingdom of God here on earth. Reading the Bible always is so exciting because you will come across so many things that were unknown to you to live a worthwhile life on earth rather than a wasteful one, in wise ideas, practice, time and spirituality.

On the Judgement Day who will have some points to support the evil ways they were doing on earth? Who will declare ignorance of what they were expected to do to please their creator? Read what Paul teaches to humanity: ROMANS 1:18-32; 2:1-16. A day spent in penitence and forgiveness by God is commendable for one who is serious to enter heaven to live with the Lord forever and ever. Such a day is so important because it gives hope for salvation. God's award to the saved one which is "Eternal life" is much, much greater and significant than any amount of money. God gives an award to the victorious people that no man on earth can give.

The writer might sound speaking Greek to non-Greek speaking people because the concealed truth is hard to excavate like the gold hidden underground where there are darkness and rocky obstacles that need light and dynamites to have access to it.

In self-defence, when waging war against the evil one, Paul advises us in **Ephesians 6:10–18** what we ought to do with the help of the Lord. We have to put on "the Armour of God" in fighting the war against the devil as people, having an ambition to rise above culture in our daily living. *"Put on the full armour of God, so that you can take your stand against the devil's schemes for our struggle is not against flesh and blood, but against the rulers, against the authorities, against the powers of this dark world and against the spiritual forces of evil in heavenly realms."*

Armour of God

1. The belt of truth around the waist
2. The breastplate of righteousness
3. The Gospel of peace
4. The shield of faith
5. The helmet of salvation
6. The sword of the Spirit which is the word of God

With the advice to us by Paul, we can rise above culture and have a culture controlled by God who is righteous and loving. God's principles are very high for human beings but we can do our best to observe them. Noah, Abraham, Jacob, Joseph, Moses, Joshua, David the prophets of God and Jesus' Apostles succeeded with the help of God. If they made it, we can make it with the help of Jesus who knows no defeat. Like what Julius Caesar wrote when he had won a battle in Eraque, "veni, vidi, vinci" meaning

"I came, I saw, I conquered." We, Christians today, can enter the battle field led by Jesus with a motto: "venitemus; videtemus; vincemus" meaning: 'We will come; we will see; we will conquer. We take God's order to Joshua as the order to us. JOSHUA **1:7–8** reads thus: *"Be strong and very courageous. Be careful to obey all the law my servant Moses gave you; do not turn from it to the right or to the left, that you may be successful wherever you go. Keep this Book of the Law always on your lips; meditate on it day and night, so that you may be careful to do everything written in it. Then you will be prosperous and successful."*

Through obedience to God, the Israelites travelled from the house of bondage in Egypt to the Promised Land, the land of freedom through thick and thin. In the same way Christians should have the same faith and courage to reach the heavenly permanent home, Jesus being the spiritual leader as He said, *"I am the way and the truth and the life. No one comes to the Father except through me"* JOHN **14:6**.

The Christian believers who have been called to evangelise people in the world are doing what they were instructed to do to win souls for Christ. However, it seems there are more people lacking integrity to rely on or to be employable in some places and as a result profits, gains or products deteriorate. When businesses operate like this, they quickly go bankrupt. Where people are honest and diligent, production is stable or increases. Some people say where employees are underpaid, they lack motivation to work diligently to the detriment of the company. In this case, conditions of services need to be examined and improved. If working conditions are bad to the employees, there will come temptations that will force some workers to behave in unbecoming ways and rising above culture at work place, becomes a challenge.

Chapter 5

PEOPLE AS STEWARDS OF THEMSELVES AND OTHER CREATURES

A steward is a person who is given the responsibility to look after movable or immovable property. They can care for people and other created things properly as managers. In the creation story, a person was made a steward of the created things like human beings, animals and plants. In GENESIS 1:26 we read thus: *"Then God said "Let us make mankind in our image, in our likeness, so that they may rule over the fish in the sea and the birds in the sky, over the livestock and all the wild animals, and even all the creatures that move along the ground."* Since creatures depend on plants, weeds, water, soil and water, these too need to be looked after carefully for the welfare of insects, birds, animals and human beings – God's stewards. If no good stewardship is practiced, people themselves, animals, plants, soil and air lose their values. Wild animals move from one place to another in search of good pasture, Plants will not grow well because of land degradation and drought. Some trees and grass are cut down or burnt unnecessarily by human beings. The top soil is washed away by water into rivers causing siltation. The animals that live in the rivers are driven to extinction because water is polluted.

When natural vegetations are affected adversely by water, soil erosion is likely to take place. Desertification will deface the land upon which animate animals depend. Such natural phenomena can result in starvation and poverty among the people who dwell in those places. The stewards of the created things might just watch things under their responsibility, deteriorating as if it is the normal way things should happen. The citizens in a place or country, might look to the government to take action to curb the ongoing deterioration of the land and vegetation. In such circumstances, there are people who fail to rise above culture to prevent the destruction of land, vegetation and animals on land and in water.

The stewards who rise above culture are those who are aware of their responsibilities to make the land natural and habitable. Such stewards work to reclaim the gullies, stop soil erosion by growing plants like trees and grass where the land is bare. This can be the responsibility of an institution like the government, farmers or people who dwell in those places as the land will be occupied by their descendants. The present stewards should bear in mind of the welfare of the people coming after them – this is to be responsible. In some places where there were animals of different kinds, they are now nowhere to be found. Clever stewards might have big and small animals in the game parks and reserves; for the people to see the actual animals rather pictures of animals only. Integrity, diligence, commitment and sacrifice in carrying out the work that is supposed to be done for mutual good, can make the good stewards rise above culture to the joy of people and to the glory of the creator. Schools, churches, governments should take the lead in training people to be good stewards of animals, water, soil, vegetation and air to the joy of the creator and the animate creatures.

The air we breathe in is polluted especially, in the heavily industrialised places. Scientists, engineers and industrialists must find ways of curbing pollution of the air on which plants, animals and people depend. To rise above culture to please God and the people who are stewards, is to curb air pollution by using electricity mostly. Air pollution results in climatic changes that will affect animate animals, people and plants adversely. People hold meetings about the danger of air pollution but solutions are slow to come up, to rise above culture. Stewards who rise above culture are engaged in how the things ought to be done with more advantages than disadvantages to people and other animate creatures as favourable environments are put in place. God is responsible and so should people be as the Lord's stewards, to placate God through their deeds.

Stewards should obey their employer who is theologically, the creator of all things in heaven and on earth. God created things "ex nihilo" 'out of nothing.' He spoke and things came into existence. The Word, "O Logos" that was spoken is Jesus, the Word incarnate, Immanuel mentioned in the Gospel according to **John 1:1–3** *"In the beginning was Word and the Word was with God, and the Word was God. He was with God in the beginning. Through him all things were made without him nothing was made that has been made."* These words in the Gospel according to John, throw light on the words in Genesis 1 where it is said, "In the beginning God created the heaven and the earth. Now the earth was formless and empty, darkness was over the surface of the deep, and the Spirit of God was hovering over the waters. God the Father, God the Holy Spirit and the Word, Jesus or God the Son are co-eternal as Persons in the Triune God. In **Genesis 1:3**, it is said, *"God said, "Let there be light."* God spoke the Word for the light to come into existence, the natural phenomenon that science or philosophy cannot explain because this is beyond human comprehension. There are truths that can be comprehended by faith and truths that can be comprehended by philosophy and science through reasoning and experiments in the realm of human beings. God's activities about the origin of animate and inanimate things are in the heavenly realm of the supernatural Being who is invisible, spiritual and immortal. Things that happen in the heavenly realm can be understood through faith revealed to mankind by God hence in Christianity we have doctrines of creation, revelation, incarnation (The Word becoming flesh through the immaculate conception of the Virgin Mary for our sake, to be saved from sin and eternal death), the doctrine of God, Christology, Reconciliation, ecclesiology, soteriology and eschatology. These doctrines explain the Christian faith in a clear, coherent and consistent way in the Christian Theology (Theos– God, and Logos (reason). This is the clear reasoning about God and His relationship to things under His charge as the Sovereign Ruler and Almighty God (El Shaddai), Everlasting God (El Olam).

Human beings who are God's stewards, are under God who enables the former to wake up in the morning, to live, work and procreate as is said in **Genesis 1:28**, *"God blessed them and said to them, "Be fruitful and increase in number, fill the earth and subdue it. Rule over the fish in the sea and the* *birds in the sky and living creature that move on the ground."* Human beings, God's image (imago Dei) ought to obey God, the Owner of all things in the universe. Power to rule over fellow people and other creatures animate and inanimate was given to them to use appropriately and responsibility with justice, love and empathy. Rulers are like employed shepherds who look after the many sheep and yet they are not the owners. They cannot market them without the consent of the owners who bought them to rear. They do not make any decisions to slaughter them for meat because the decision lies with the owners of the sheep. The shepherds are only workers doing the shepherding on behalf of the owners according to the division of labour. People of integrity are supposed to rule over others in fear of God who is loving, just and righteous. If God's will is not followed by the rulers, there is no peace in the land under their jurisdiction. Rulers should avoid corruption, envy, selfishness, cruelty and other types of immoralities because they are against the will of God. To fear God is to rise above culture because God is perfect and people who profess to be children of God by rebirth, as explained in JOHN 1:12, *"yet to all who did receive him, to those who believed in his name, he gave the right to become children of God – children born not of natural descent, nor of human decision or a husband's will, but born of God",* should be obedient to God.

Rulers who are also stewards of God, should be humble, polite and loving. They should not play bosses over the people who elect them into power but servant leaders as the title "Prime Minister" is derived from two Latin words. 'Prime' is derived from the Latin word 'Primus' which means 'first' in English and the word 'Minister' is a Latin word meaning an attendant servant, assistant or pastor, from the Latin word 'minor' meaning 'less' as a servant is of a less status than the employer or the one whom he serves according to theological standards, as it is implied in LUKE 22:27 *"For who is greater, the one who is at the table or the one who serves? Is it not the one who is at the table? But I am among you as one who serves."* Jesus, the teacher and Lord who created heaven and earth became a servant of people He created. This shows humility and love for people created in the image of God. To rise above culture, this is how the rulers should behave to the people under their charge. If Jesus, did it, why can't we as His followers? rulers are only God's representatives to execute justice and promote righteousness and peace among the people. The Prime Minister, therefore is the "First Servant" of the people and the "ministers" are the servants of the people representing them in the parliament to express their will and make laws on their behalf. They listen to the "voice of the people", "Vox Populi" if they are democratic, if they become dictators, they will ignore "Vox Populi" in favour of their desires. This is when the rulers perform below the mark in an exploitative way to please themselves rather than the people who elected them into power through their franchise. Doing the will of God to the people or for the people is what the rulers should do to promote love, kindness, unity and peace for progress and prosperity of the nation. Rulers should work for the people as they rule for the common good, that is, for their good also. The rulers should work hard to narrow the gap between the have and the have not. The unemployed, the sick, the disabled, the elderly and the needy are the responsibility of the government under the ministry or service of Social Services and Development. The churches and other charitable organisations come in to assist the needy as is meant in Jesus' parable of "The Good Samaritan" in the Gospel of Luke **10:25-37**. People with mental health challenge should not be neglected and left to wander about but they should be cared for as we are our brothers' and sisters' keepers. Let us not be like Cain in the Bible who denied his responsibility for his brother Abel, when God asked him the whereabouts of his brother whom he had killed and buried in the ground as narrated in Genesis **4:8-11**, The Holy Bible says, *"Now Cain said to his brother Abel, "Let's go out to the field. While they were in the field, Cain attacked his brother Abel and killed him." Then the Lord said to Cain, "Where is your brother Abel?" "I don't know," he replied. "Am I my brother's keeper?" The Lord said, "what have you done? Listen! Your brother's blood cries out to me from the ground. Now you are under a curse and driven from the ground which opened its mouth to receive your brother's blood from your hand."* God is omniscient and omnipresent. All human secrets are known by Him and He judges in righteousness. The ill-treatment and the benevolent acts you do to a fellow person is seen and known by God and you will give an account of what you did to God one day as is said in **MATTHEW 12:36** *"But I tell you that everyone will have to give account on the day of judgement for every empty word they have spoken. For by your words, you will be condemned."* In **MATTHEW 25:31–46** Jesus explained the judgement of people metaphorically as the separation of the sheep from the goats, showing that the good or the bad you do to your fellow person, you do to God and the verdict will be passed according to what you did. The judgement of God is two sided. On one side is justification and on the other side is condemnation. Jesus who is the Saviour in our time will come as the Judge of all the nations during his Parousia or the second coming. We should not pretend to be innocent for the sinful things we do to the others. We should confess our sins and repent so that we can be forgiven by God and made righteous by Him as taught by Jesus in the Parable of "The Prodigal Son" found in the Gospel according to **LUKE 15:11–32**.

To rise above culture in light of God is to fear God, that is to obey, honour and love God which makes us to be humble before Him, in our vertical relationship with Him. In our horizontal relationship with our fellow people, we should remember what we do to them, we do God. We should love them as we love ourselves. We should be fair to them to please God. We should love even those who hate us as is said by Peter in **1 PETER 3:9** *"Do not repay evil with evil or insult with insult. On the contrary, repay evil with blessing, because to this you were called so that you may inherit a blessing."* Earlier on Jesus said, *"you have heard that it was said, 'Love your neighbour and hate your enemy.' But I tell you, love your enemies and pray for those who persecute you that you may be children of your Father in Heaven. He causes the sun to rise on the evil and the good, and sends rain on the righteous and the unrighteous"* **MATTHEW 5:43–45**. Jesus, the Son of God, agreed with His Father in His teachings and deeds. Therefore, those who choose to rise above culture must take Jesus' teachings seriously although some of His teachings seem to be very difficult to do because that is the will of God and we were created for Him to do His will on earth as it is done in heaven.

Christian education

The word of God is food for the soul, the inner person and the mind. Human beings can retrieve the lost sanity by reading the word of God and understand it. In the Bible study we have the cognitive aspect to be covered, that is the acquisition of knowledge of things written in the Bible. The cognitive aspect is followed by affective aspect which is the use of the knowledge acquired in the cognitive aspect to influence our attitudes and behaviour for the better. The affective aspect is finally followed by the application aspect where faith is put into action to yield good results for the self and others in the society to the glory of God, our Creator. The foretaste of heavenly life should be experienced here and now on earth as we hope to have perfect life hereafter in heaven where there is no tempter nor sin. This teaching was brought about as "Realised Eschatology" by some known theologians like J.A.T Robinson, Joachim Jeremias, Ethelbert Staviffer (1902– 1979) and C.H. David (1884– 1973). Through Jesus Christ the Kingdom of Heaven was realised on earth and people have to enter it without any delay. Those who enter it should behave as citizens and children of God who have adopted a culture of the Kingdom of God. When Jesus Christ resurrected from the dead, He appeared to His disciples and taught them about the Kingdom of God **Acts 1:3** *"After his suffering, he presented himself to them and gave them convincing proofs that he was alive. He appeared to them over a period of forty days and spoke about the Kingdom of God."* In **Luke 17:20–21**, Jesus indicated the kingdom of God that the Pharisees were expecting to come on earth and yet to them it was yet to come in the future. He said, *"The coming of the Kingdom of God is not something that can be observed, nor will people say, 'Here it is' or 'There it is,' because the Kingdom of God is in your midst."* This means that Jesus Himself was the King and the Kingdom of God had then been established by Him. The Kingdom of God is to be entered here on earth through repentance, baptism and acceptance of Jesus as the Lord and Saviour. In **1 Corinthians 12:3** Paul said *"Therefore I want you to know that no one who is speaking by the Spirit of God says, Jesus be cursed, and no one can say, "Jesus is Lord except by the Holy Spirit."* The Kingdom is here on earth where we should live as saved people through Jesus who suffered and died on the cross vicariously for our sins. This Kingdom of God will be consummated in heaven.

The eschatological teachings are theologically, not philosophically nor scientifically explained. Those who believe accept the teachings as apocalyptic and real for they will happen in the future but now we have the foretaste of what will happen in full in the absence of the tempter.

In teleological ethics we learn that people aim at the goal and when the goal is reached, happiness ensues. In Christianity, the goal is salvation from sin and eternal death which starts from the earth and completed in heaven when one is ultimately justified by God to enter heaven (JOHN 3:16). The judgement of God that is coming is not for animals but for human beings as they have conscience to choose what is right from wrong, good from bad, just or unjust, what to take or what not to take. The Judgement will be based on one's choices or deeds.

In writing this book, the writer feels strongly that he has an obligation to give the awareness to people that we people are not our own creators but there is one much greater, who created us in His image whom we should obey and always seek to do His will to live in harmony with Him here on earth and hereafter in heaven. We cannot be perfect on our own by doing good things only. Faith connects us to God and good works, should be the fruits of our faith. The stewards of God, the human beings and the other creatures of which we are custodians are God's, the Sovereign Ruler. To rise above culture, one has to adapt to the principles that are in line with the Supernatural Being for whom we were created. Choosing what is good or bad, right or wrong, will help us to live responsibly in the society or rise above culture.

Jesus and Culture

Learning from Jesus, the Word incarnate, the only begotten Son of God and the perfect revelation of God to mankind who taught mankind to rise above culture, we can see how rising above culture can be done for the liberation, joy and social development of people who are stewards of God.

Jesus was a Jew, a descendent of King David. His earthly parents were Jews, yet the Son of God, by God's miraculous plan (Luke 1:26–38). He was raised up as a Jew following the Jewish customs for His physical, social, intellectual, and spiritual development. He went to a synagogue school where he studied and enlightened His teachers on the scriptures to their surprise. Jesus was presented in the Temple (Luke 2:22–40). When Jesus was twelve years old, His parents went up to the Temple in Jerusalem for the festival, according to the custom (Luke 2:42). Jesus was respectful to His parents (Luke 2:49–51). We can see how Jesus developed spiritually, physically and socially in His relationship with God and people within the Jewish culture (Luke 2:52). Jesus was humble to be baptised by John the Baptist and yet He is the Son of God (Luke 3:21–23); (John 1:29–34). Religion is part of a culture but revelations in that custom come from the Supernatural Being, the creator of heaven and earth who is holy. The creator wants people made in His image to be holy or righteous like Him through faith and by His grace. For Christians, perfection is through faith in Jesus, the Immanuel who became like us yet truly God and truly man through the incarnation. Jesus chose to die for the people's sins for their salvation from sin and eternal death (John 3:16).

Within His culture, Jesus taught, preached and healed people when He performed miracles as the signs of God's presence among the people. He ate and mixed with other people at a wedding and funerals and raised the dead (Luke 7:11–17; Mark 5:21–24, 35–43; John 11:1–44). During the time of Jesus, there were no hospitals like the ones we have today but faith healing was commonly used. God manifested His presence through miracles. Those who believed in God, were empowered by God Himself to cure diseases. This cultural practice was extended to Jesus' Apostles and to today's Christians who believe in faith healing as well as scientific healing where medicines are used in hospitals. The Christians believe that doctors and medicines are God's. The doctors as human beings are endowed with the mental capacity to heal even if some of them do not believe in God because God's love is universal and unconditional. The medicines used by doctors are extracted from plants created by God but mixed scientifically according to scientific measures to cure ailments. All people are God's people or children by creation through natural status that does not qualify them to enter heaven without the spiritual rebirth, according to the Christian faith but qualifies them to have human rights on earth. To qualify to enter heaven according to the Christian teachings, to rise above culture through rebirth spiritually is of necessity (JOHN 1:12–13; 3:1–15) to become children of God by adoption and coheirs with Jesus in eternity as stated in ROMANS 8:17, *"Now if we are children, then we are heirs – heirs of God and co–heirs with Christ, if indeed we share in his sufferings in order that we may also share in his glory"*.

When Jesus was an adult, after His baptism by John the Baptist, he was ready to carry out the ministry that God His Father sent Him for in the world (JOHN 4:1–44; 5:1–39; 6:1–49; 7:1–50; 8:1–56; 1:62; 10:1–42; 11:1–53; 12:1–59 AND CHAPTERS 13 –24). Jesus was tempted by the devil with what could create cheap popularity to Him because He was truly man and truly God. The devil failed to convince Him because He was not only man but also God and invincible. God cannot be defeated by His creatures like the devil himself, a prohibited immigrant in heaven (REVELATION 12:7–17).

Some of theologians say the opportune time the devil was again waiting for to tempt Jesus was, one of the most difficult times in the life of Jesus (LUKE 4:13). These opportune times came when Jesus was in Gethsemane making the final decision of His fate LUKE 22:42; when He was standing before Herod for trial and was asked to play a role of a clown to entertain Herod. Herod wanted Jesus to perform miracles for entertainment and yet miracles were meant to be the signs of the presence of God (LUKE 23:8–12) and when Jesus was on the cross, the climax of His physical suffering, a shameful and very painful suffering for false crimes which led to Jesus' vicarious death for the sins of humanity, (LUKE 23:32–49), Jesus could have escaped sufferings and death on the cross but He decided to stick to His mission He was sent for on earth by God, His Father. In His life, Jesus worked hard to help the people to rise above culture through teachings, preaching, miracles and his own personal life. His sermon on the mount,

(Matthew chapters 5 to 7) was practical. He encouraged his followers to put faith into action for their faith to be real and different from that of the Pharisees and Sadducees. He wanted his followers to be the salt and light of the world in thought, word and deed. In the fulfilment of God's Law to the people, Jesus explained the Law that was at times, misinterpreted or exaggerated and fulfilled it even in His life. Such teachings of Jesus truly motivated impenitent sinners to be penitent as they were given healthy food for the spirit and mind to rise above culture in any society, what is right ought to be promoted but what is wrong in the sight of God is to be abandoned for our mutual good and salvation on earth. Just as we do not want to eat any type of food but choose what to eat, the same applies to the spiritual food that is put before us by the world. There are times when people choose what they eat and what they should not eat for their health physically. Naturally and voluntarily, people eat what they choose to eat as they choose to be responsible or irresponsible.

The writer, in his discourse on rising above culture, is to choose that which is good, right or just and discard the negative for individual and collective welfare as people created in the image of God and as we cohabit in one land that God created. This concept in theological ethics is also found in philosophical ethics of utilitarianism that supports the common good coupled with meta ethics which supports the decision or choice made in light of the authority backing it, May what the writer has put down in black and white influence any reader who may single out even one idea to put into practice for one's unselfish good or for the common good in any society or world as we try to please our Maker, so that we rise above culture in this world that God declared to be good when He created it– **Genesis 1:31**, *"God saw all that he had made, and it was very good. And there was evening, and there was morning– the sixth day."*

Marriage

Reflecting on the social institution of marriage theologically, it is God's plan for humanity to bring persons of their likeness in the world. Heterosexual marriage promotes the divine and continuous creation of God's people through procreation (**Genesis 1:27–31**). Marriage is a mysterious union of two people of opposite gender to fulfil God's plan and therefore adults intending to get married should take serious vows before their creator and witnesses during the occasion to be together as life partners in fear of God the Sovereign Ruler by observing the theological principles that lead to good marriage (**Genesis 1:18, 20 –24, Matthew 19:3–12**). The two persons joined in holy matrimony become one flesh, living in harmony and focused on God, for the fulfilment of His plan for their good and that of humanity.

Violation of God's plan brings about many problems like marriage breakdown, self-imposed single life, temptations that lead to sexual immorality, procreation outside marriage, neglected children who may lack parental, spiritual and moral training, drunkenness and use of drugs by the neglected children in their attempt to avert some life-threatening social evils like lack of love, hunger, poverty, abuse, homelessness and discrimination. Marriage should be protected for procreation, fellowship and economic sustenance in the society. The theological principles of agape love, respect and faithfulness should be strictly observed. This mysterious institution of marriage in a family of two persons, a husband and a wife and a couple with children should be guarded jealously so that children can be nurtured carefully to adulthood. Parents should avoid temptations of running away from their parental responsibilities to their children, given to them as gifts from God. Children need their parental love, guidance and protection until they become adults when they can stand on their own.

In marriage, a couple needs to be guided by Christian principles on morality like love, joy, peace forbearance, kindness, goodness, faithfulness, gentleness and self-control (**Galatians 5:22–23**). This teaching is there to help a couple rise above culture that is led by emotions mainly rather than reason in solving marital issues. It is difficult to see things eye to eye when two persons with different cultural backgrounds get into marriage. What is required for the two persons in life partnership, is social adaptation for better principles of living. Refusing adaptation is refusing to live meaningfully for mutual good. Such attitude and behaviour is, in most cases, attended to by chaotic moments that will disturb social fabric. To rise above culture, we should aim at maintaining social fibers designed to alleviate the conditions of poverty, to better the welfare of the couple and children. We should examine our attitudes and behaviour unbiasedly and get rid of some elements in our own subcultures that are incompatible with what we ought to do in the society. Sacrifice is required in doing anything that is good. The doing is difficult but the result, is as sweet as honey. Habitual anti–social activities may appear good to the perpetrators but at the same time they are bad and destructive to the characters and other people's welfare. It is said in **Proverbs 22:1**, *"A good name is more desirable than great riches; to be esteemed is better than silver or gold."* Such words help us to rise above culture. What we do at times is not what we ought to do. In this case, we should aim at doing better in life rather than opting to maintain the status quo to our own detriment. God is there for us all to consult for advice on social issues as King David did and succeeded (**1 Kings 3:1– 15, 2 Chronicles 1:1 –17**). There are times when we wonder in the wilderness of our minds and yet answers to our problems are so near. The Holy Bible has solutions to most of our social problems which haunt and destroy us as individuals and nations.

Family

Sociologists regard a family as a basic unit of a society. This family is a result of marriage. Therefore, marriage and a family should be seen as the two sides of the same coin. In other words, they are complementary. A well–maintained beginning of marriage, leads to a strong family. Marriage should not be based on eros love but on agape love – the former is based on attractiveness of the individuals when that which was attractive disappears, love dwindles to the extent of even a divorce whereas the latter makes marriage binding for life in its confines of legality and theological morality (**Matthew 19:8–9**). Personal beauty, handsomeness, wealth and other attractions in eros love, can be unattractive or disappear altogether to our chaotic confusion in marriage. However, agape love will help the couple to stick together in fear of God. Love, kindness, forgiveness, patience, endurance and self-control can help the couple to go on in their marriage till separated by death. Parents as the first teachers in informal education, on which formal education is built, should be resolute in teaching their children in different aspects of life. Informal education will empower children spiritually, morally, physically, psychologically, economically and socially. Parents should not abandon their children to the care of the misleading peer groups. Children should be taught carefully when they are still young to be responsible people in the society (**Proverbs 22:6**, **Isaiah 54:13**, **Proverbs 1:8–9**, **Psalm 127:3**, **Matthew 19:4**, **Proverbs 17:6**, **3 John 1:4**, **Deuteronomy 5–29**, **Ephesians 6:4**, **Matthew 18:1–3**, **Jeremiah 1:5**, **Deuteronomy 6:6–7**).

Parents should play role models to their children for them to take some of the good qualities from them for social development. They can shape up good and responsible citizens of any country to the joy of the people and the glory of God. We are our brothers', husbands', wives' children's and parents' keepers with God's help, as we aim at rising above the culture that leads to rising to eternal life after resurrection from the dead. Let us experience the existence of the Kingdom of God here on earth as the foretaste of our heavenly banquet. We worship the God of impossibilities who enables us to confront negativities and some impossibilities in life fearlessly, for He fights battles for us when they are beyond our strength and knowledge, parents should always be aware of the truth that people are waging war against invisible enemies (**Ephesians 6:12**). They should courageously uphold the motto of faith "Deus semper invictus est" – "God is always invincible or undefeated" as they are encouraged by the words in **Psalm 119:105–106** *"Your word is a lamp for my feet, a light on my path. I have taken an oath and confirmed it, that I will follow your righteous laws."*

Beware of social issues that destroy families

Temper stops people from rising above culture. It urges them to be puffed up with pride. This attitude which they adopt make them look outlandish in ideas, attitudes and behaviour at their own and other people's expense. People may try to live in their own world where other people do not matter but themselves. They work for their own development at the expense of that of others and against the natural principle of interdependence for the co-existence of people for their welfare, at times, high education acquired, might tempt persons in marriage life partnership to look down upon each other with a feeling of superiority and inferiority complex. They forget the oath they made during the solemn wedding. When one is unemployed for a long time, especially a man who is described as the head of the family, the devil can pay him many uninvited visits, to desert the family or the spouse. He seeks separation or divorce as if eros love was the foundation of marriage. Responsibilities to each other and children are discarded in search of wealth. Quickly, notice the presence of the devil when you seek to destroy the institution of marriage and the social unit of a family. Uphold the motto of awareness "Vigilate et orate" – "Watch and pray," so that the devil does not snatch you away as is said by Peter in his first letter to the persecuted Christians in Asia Minor: *"Be alert and of sober mind your enemy the devil prowls around like a roaring lion looking for someone to devour. Resist him, stand firm in the faith because you know that the family of believers throughout the world is undertaking the same kind of sufferings."* (**1 Peter 5:8–9**).

Lack of the first love caused by clandestine practices in the misuse of the family money can destroy marriage. One or both might decide to assist relatives or friends without the knowledge of the other partner. By so doing integrity is lost, development hampered and suspicion creeps into the family to cause confusion and erode trust. The money earned by the couple is first and foremost for the family. It does not matter whether one earns more money than the other. If assistance is to be given to relatives this should meet the agreement of the couple after the assessment of the need. If the need is so great and threatens life, compassion will take the lead in decision-making, Autocratic decisions in a family should be avoided as much as possible to maintain trust in the family. It is prudent for a couple to be faithful in marriage to maintain the vow made on their wedding. Unfaithfulness corrodes the love in the mysterious oneness in flesh through the sacred marriage. Sexual gratification outside marriage is adultery and a sin and destroys the social institution of marriage. The Christian virtue of self–control can save the marriage. It is in marriage where sexual gratification is justifiable and a way to promote procreation responsibly. Disobedience begets sinful practices that God hates and works to liberate humanity from. When we become obedient, we are regarded as responsible citizens of God's Kingdom here on earth. Theological sexual ethics should be adhered to if we are to rise above culture. Social norms and values ought to be preserved in every culture but the bad ones ought to be discarded to please God and people amongst whom we live. Adopting such a social practice is one of the ways to rise above culture. We should choose good social practices in a culture and abandon the bad ones.

Mutual respect in a marriage or family should be enjoyed between the husband and his wife. This respect should spill over the whole family where there are children so that the children also know how family life is lived when they become adults. This is informal education to be practiced in the society for people's social development and prosperity in various ways. Nobody likes to be disrespected and embarrassed publicly or privately. All people would like to preserve their dignity that makes them feel equal to any other person in the society.

It is a bad habit to get involved in gossiping in any social groups (EPHESIANS 4:29, PROVERBS 6:16–19, PROVERBS 21:23, JAMES 1:26, PROVERBS 20:19, MATTHEW 12:36, PSALM 34:13, TITUS 3:2, PROVERBS 18:8, PROVERBS 26 :20). The word of God encourages us to be trustworthy in speech and deeds in the family.

All in all, discipline is required in the family as people aiming to live above culture in any society. Deeds will distinguish a good family from the bad one as is said, "actions speak louder than words." Constant lessons in social studies will help adults and children grow up as responsible people in the society. It is not too late for anyone to abandon bad social practices and rise above culture as liberated people who deserve respect and people's dependability.

Third culture children and their future

The writer has in mind the present and future of the third culture children in diaspora where their parents have a home original cultural background which is different from the prevalent culture, in the country they are currently living. There are children born and brought up in a new environment now almost if not completely detached from that of the original country of the parents. Automatically there is a language barrier to communicate meaningfully with their relatives in some places in their parents' motherland. Is there any possibility to provide means to bridge the original and the second culture as they get adopted to the third culture?

The children ought to rise above culture to remain contactable in all cultures so that they do not lose their identity. They have to learn the original parental culture the new culture of the people they live amongst and adopt the third culture which is a mixture of the original and adopted culture to interact with the two groups. This approach of living in a pluralistic world will make racial intermarriages helpful. Because of urbanisation, migratory labour and migration on different grounds, people from different countries are where they are today. Some people had hoped to be where they are for a short period of time which ends up a miscalculation of the intended duration of their stay. Now, maybe, the intention they intended to fulfil is now water under the bridge. The option left for them is to leave permanently where they are and visit relatives back home when chances occur.

The children born in foreign lands must make up their minds to marry or to be married where they are according to decisions based on imperative ethics, that is where they ought to marry or alternatively, using situational ethics, that is, where it is fitting to marry and enter cultural or interracial marriages if advantages outweigh disadvantages in each case. Martin Luther King Jnr, once said, a person should be judged by his or her character, not by skin colour. There is no place in the life of the Christian for favouritism based on race (JAMES 2:1–10). He went further to say, when selecting a mate, a Christian should first find out if the potential spouse is born again by faith in Jesus Christ (JOHN 3:3–5). Faith in Christ not skin colour is the biblical standard for choosing a spouse. Interracial marriage is not a matter of right or wrong but of wisdom, discernment and prayer. In the Bible we read that Joseph, the dreamer, an Israelite, got married to Asenath, the daughter of Potiphar, priest from the city of an Egyptian, (**Genesis 41:45**). He was the mother of Manasseh and Ephraim (**Genesis 41:50, 46:20**). Ruth a Moabite woman married a Jew, Boaz and became one of Jesus gentile ancestors. Moses an Israelite married an Ethiopian wife Zipporah.

Our contemporaries, former president of the United States of America Barack Obama is a son of a Kenyan Barack Obama Snr and his mother was S. Ann Dunham, the former president of Botswana the son of Seretse Khama of Botswana an African and Ruth Williams a white lady. It takes wisdom from God and a discerning spirit in any culture for one to rise above culture irrespective of culture or race. God has good plans for all people in the world which keep on unfolding as they live contrary to their expectations. The life we live today has been lived by some people who have lived before us, as history repeats itself in one way or another.

Widows and widowers

In spite that widows and widowers lost their life partners owing to the natural phenomenon of death, they have very important roles to play in the society. They can take up leadership roles in the places of employment and worship in the church. Their influence in their leadership can influence people in many aspects of life, to rise above culture in their attitudes and behaviour. They have the right to remarry or remain single (**1 Corinthians 7:39**). Paul teaches about caring for widows and those in need (**1 Timothy 5:3 –16**). Widowers, widows and the aged people ought to be given assistance spiritually, morally, materially and financially to raise their standard of living. We are our brothers' and sisters' keepers. The horizontal relationship between the 'have and the have not' is encouraged in the Bible for the giver to rise above culture (**Acts 20:35, Luke 6:38, Hebrews 13 :16, Exodus 22:22**).

Orphans in the society

People are urged to care for the orphans, (**James 1:27, James 2:15 –16, Hosea 14:3, Isaiah 1:17, Psalm 8 2, 3, Deuteronomy 10:18, John 29:12, John 14:18**).

In **Psalm 68:5** it is written, *"As father to the fatherless a defender of the widows, is God in his holy dwelling."* Those who were inspired by God, are moved to care for the fatherless for them to grow normally like those who have their fathers. In **Exodus 22:22–24**, God says to the people, *"Do not take advantage of the widow or the fatherless. If you do and they cry out to me, I will be aroused, and I will kill you with the sword, your wives will become widows and your children will become fatherless."* God has compassion over the orphans. Those who hear the word of God and put it into practice rise above culture because they care for the needy and the vulnerable.

The answers to most of the social problems have been given to mankind in the Holy Bible. This reminds the writer of the song titled, **"There is a balm in Gilead."**

> There is a balm in Gilead
> To make the wounded whole
> There is a balm in Gilead
> To heal the sin sick soul
>
> Sometimes I feel discouraged
> And deep I feel the pain.
> In prayers the Holy Spirit
> Revives my soul again.
>
> There is a balm in Gilead
> To make the wounded whole
> There is a balm in Gilead
> To heal the sin– sick soul.
>
> If you can't pray like Peter
> If you can't be like Paul,
> Go home and tell your neighbour
> He died to save us all
>
> There is a balm in Gilead
> To make the wounded whole
> There is a balm in Gilead
> To heal the wounded soul

God is at work with His people

The God of Abraham, Isaac and Jacob is the Father of our Lord Jesus who can help us rise above the culture, to act responsibly in any society, we may find ourselves. Through obedience to God and translation of our faith into action, we can transform the world into a better world to live in and where the dignity of life is highly valued. To obey God or to have faith in God is to live in fellowship with the triune God who is everywhere. He can be contacted anywhere and at any time for guidance, comfort, protection and encouragement, as we travel the life journey whose way is Jesus, the Son of God and the perfect revelation of God the Father. As we travel this journey, we should not expect to meet good situations only because the devil is at work also. We should expect to meet some unnecessary roadblocks mounted by the devil. The spiritual stamped passport of faith is Jesus. When we reach the devil's roadblocks, the devil himself will be scared to see our passports and quickly take to his heels. James the brother of our Lord Jesus wrote in his letter advising the believers in Christ what to do when confronted by the devil. He said, *"Submit yourselves, then, to God. Resist the devil, and he will flee from you."* The devil is scared by the believers' spiritual status for he finds them impeccable and well protected inside and outside. In the gospel of JOHN **15:5**, Jesus said to his followers, *"I am the vine, you are the branches. If you remain in me and I in you, you will bear much fruit, apart from me you can do nothing."* Power to do God's work as we rise above culture emanates from Jesus and his power scares the devil. This power from Jesus enables the believers to perform miracles of deliverance from psychological, spiritual and physical bondages. Faith healing is possible through faith in Jesus. Healing is done believers by using instruments of faith in God, prayers and fasting. The church has been given this power to pray for any social situations. The invisible God intervenes to affect the healing as is clearly stated by Peter in the book of ACTS **3:16**, *"By faith in the name of Jesus, this man whom you see and know was made strong. It is Jesus' name and the fate that comes through him that has completely healed him, as you can all see."* We should never, never doubt the presence of God in all our ecclesiastical activities, for without

Him we cannot do anything to fulfil our mission in the world that needs to be done for the liberation of mankind from different types of bondages (**Luke 4:18–19**). The mission of Jesus is the mission of the church as the chosen ones, the disciples and apostles of Jesus –the word "disciple" is from Latin word "discipilus" singular and "discipili," disciples, plural. The followers of Jesus are continuously learners of Jesus so they can be like their teacher. The disciples and apostles (aposteloi) – messengers (from the Greek word 'apostelos' messenger and 'apostelo' (verb) meaning I send, should go into the world to preach the good news about Jesus who came to liberate humanity from sin and eternal death through his death on the cross. Salvation is through faith in Jesus and by God's grace (**John 3:16**). The messengers of Jesus, should teach the word of God in depth and explain it clearly by using their acquired knowledge about God and his Kingdom; Jesus and his redemption of sinners; second birth by water and the Spirit and life after death through faith in Jesus and by God's grace. The messengers of Jesus who are like a house built on the hill, should restlessly work as they feel intrinsic motivation to serve the Lord and the people.

There should be no time wasted in the propagation of the word of God because our time on earth is very short. This time, is the time of grace which should be utilised carefully. This time of grace is mentioned in the text that Jesus Christ read in the synagogue in Nazareth found in the gospel according to (**Luke 4:19**), to proclaim the year of the Lord's favour. This is the period when sinners can be forgiven from their sins if they confess their sins and repent wholeheartedly. Those who know what will happen at the end of this known time will not take the word of God lightly. The Holy Bible is not like a novel, it is the inspired word of God for our salvation. Let us take deep interest in reading and studying this word of God with understanding. We should not just read it like what the Ethiopian eunuch was doing in his chariot (**Acts 9:30–38**).

The divine University College of God, is here on earth and it enrolls people of all ages to take their studies about God and His teachings from the book of Genesis to the book of Revelation. The triune God is the most highly qualified Being who inspires and helps the learners to understand His word for He knows everything. He sets the examinations; He marks the papers and awards marks to determine those who have succeeded and those who have not for they hear but do not put to practice what they hear. Faith in Jesus is the answer required from those who write their examination and by God's grace , some candidates are promoted to live with Lord eternally in a place where there are no suffering, ailments, hunger, death and weeping (REVELATION 21:4) but there is eternal joy in that land where the Lord God will be the light of heaven and time cannot be calculated (REVELATION 22:5).This is the place where we are heading to if we cling to our faith in Jesus during this last period of sanctification by the Holy Spirit till our departure from earth.

The word of God is the truth of God that directs us to God Himself as we were created for Him, that is why we call Him Lord because He owns us. Because He lives, we live not only on earth but eternally, for Him to be the God of the people forever. This is why the prophetic word in the Bible says that the God we worship is the God of Abraham, Isaac and Jacob meaning that He is the God of the living people. The messengers of God should always trust in God and let their faith kindle their hope to meet Him ultimately face to face. The God our Lord is already here on earth and is in control of all our life situations.

No situation can be said to be out of control of God. Things can only be out of control of human beings because their power and knowledge are limited no matter how educated they may be. Believers, like other people, can have hard times, get ill, be humiliated, attacked, killed and die. In all these situations, God is still in control. Things move according to God's plans for a purpose which we can interpret to be positive or negative. Paul in his letter to the (ROMANS 14:8) says, "*If we live, we live for the Lord, and if we die, we die for the Lord. So, whether we live or die, we belong to the Lord.*" This is very encouraging to those who believe in God. This gets rid of the fears we have about ourselves that give us sleepless nights at times. Jesus once said words of encouragement to His followers who were worrying about things that they thought they should have like other people and they constantly lived in fear of their future on earth. They feared to live in poverty or destitution. Jesus who was their leader and protector was in control of their situation. He could provide their needs but He told them to seek first the Kingdom of God and its righteousness. Do the first things first and the other things needed in life will be supplied by Jehovah Jireh. Things like food, clothes, dwelling paces are social necessities and people have to work for them. However, the most important things have been given to us by God like life and body. These other things are also provided by God since He knows that we need them. Believers in God are safe alive or dead.

The mind of having competition in possessions should be discarded but that of self-improvement within one's means should be promoted. Jesus said to his disciples then and today, *"Do not be afraid of those who kill the body but cannot kill the soul. Rather be afraid of one who can destroy both soul and body in hell. Are not two sparrows sold for a penny? Yet not one of them will fall to the ground outside your Father's care. And even the very hairs of your head are all numbered so do not be afraid, you are worth more than sparrows"* (**MATTHEW 10 :28 –31**). The Lord gives hope to the hopeless so that they can keep on moving to the promised heavenly home where there is joy and perfection. Be prepared to experience sacrifices in your life as you serve God and the people. Problems are not to be sought, let them come in response to your good work to God and the people as what happened to Jesus.

The good you do in the name of Jesus might not be accepted by some of the people who may have ulterior motives but do not be discouraged or fear those who can destroy the body but cannot destroy your soul. Love those who love you and even those who hate you for this is what God does to all the people he created in His image. This means believers and unbelievers are people of God, the former are children of God by adoption through acceptance of Jesus as their personal Saviour and the latter are children of God by creation who need a rebirth symbolised by baptism with water and the Spirit to be given the right by God to be called children of God, born of God not by the decision of a human being (JOHN 1:12–13). The prophet Isaiah earlier on encouraged the believers in God by saying, *"But those who hope in the Lord will renew their strength. They will soar on wings like eagles, they will run and not grow weary, they will walk and not be faint"* (ISAIAH 40:31). God strengthens His people who hope for their salvation in Him, to keep on serving Him tirelessly for them to be saved from sin and eternal death. Those who are truly called by God will be restless until they fulfil the call by doing what God tells them to do counting not the cost. Find joy in serving God and the people who should be liberated from sin that leads to death. The call of God is experienced as an imperative personal passion, initiated by God for one called to serve God Himself and the people to be saved.

Prayerful life as a necessity for the chosen ones

Jesus Christ who was truly man and truly God on earth, took time to pray to God to remain connected to Him. Dialogue with the Father was necessary in the achievement of his goals on earth. In the desert when He was making some preparations to save mankind, Satan appeared to Him and tempted Him. Satan could not dissuade Jesus because He agreed with God His Father in the salvific plan for humanity. Jesus cited the scriptures to silence Satan in His temptations. As Jesus was in the garden of Gethsemane, He prayed to His Father to reach the logical conclusion about His fate as enemies where about to apprehend Him for accusations they had laid upon Him. Jesus could pray alone and with or among His followers which is a normal thing to do in a family, fellowship and in general.

Jesus set an example to His followers on what the worshippers or believers in God should do to maintain a good relationship with the Father. Right relationship with God brings peace of mind to the believer. Through prayer, the believer's heart is strengthened by the power of the Holy Spirit. Consistent prayer releases the power of God's blessings on the life and circumstances of a believer. Conversation in prayers with God is very necessary for the development of the believer's spirituality and morality. Prayers to God give the believers courage to carry out their mission with confidence for when the believers draw close to God, He draws near to them too, to listen to the petitions to which He responds. Even at the point of death, Jesus was in communication with his Father praying for His enemies to be forgiven for their ignorance in denying and crucifying Him, their Messiah. Jesus Christ, Our perfect model of spirituality and morality rose above the Jewish and the Roman cultures in His services to the Jews and the gentiles,

God is pleased with the believers who praise Him for His greatness as they admit their dependence on Him. This is how we adore our heavenly Father whose children we are. Through prayers we can confess our sins and ask God to forgive us during the prevailing time of grace. In our daily living on earth, parents and children prefer to share ideas, advice or warn any member of the family. What we do in our families on earth is what we do in the family of God. Putting into practice what God tells us to do is to act wisely and to rise above culture in attitudes, decision making and deeds,

Jesus taught about prayer and its significance (MATTHEW 6:5–8). Here, He said, when you pray, do not be like the hypocrites. Self-righteousness that promotes a show off should be avoided. It is God whom the believers should focus on rather than on self-seeking worshippers. Deceit should be avoided. Jesus taught His followers the important things they should include in their prayers, the summary of which are in the Lord's prayer found in (LUKE 11:1–13 and MATTHEW 6:7–13). He also taught two parables on the significance of persistent praying in (LUKE 18:1–18).

Ben Simone, senior leader of a church and a pastor says in the Christian faith," You can pray to God as many times a day as you want." The Christian faith does not have a set number of times to pray. One can pray when it is convenient when one feels the need for closer connection to God. A moment to pray, the "Kairos" time is important to establish intimacy with our Lord as He is always listening. Ben Simone says," If you want to deepen your relationship with God, I suggest you start praying three times a day, when you wake up, in the afternoon and before sleeping, In the Islam faith the basic requirements to pray is five times at,

1. Sunrise
2. Noon
3. Afternoon
4. Sunset
5. Night

However, in the Islam faith, prayers are practiced at the discretion of the follower. Some Muslims are stricter than others while others cannot pray at certain times. The Jews are supposed to pray three times a day, in the morning, afternoon and evening. The Jewish prayer book Siddur has special services set down to be used during the prayer times which enable them to have better relationship with God. "When one seeks a close relationship with God one has the desire to rise above culture spiritually and morally to please God. Like in secular games, there is need for participants to be disciplined to perform well. Constant practice by players or doers tends to perfect them to the joy of the onlookers and those who employ them or believe in the Christian faith, as predestined by God Himself (**Romans 8:29–30**) what they should observe and do for them to be able to make disciples of Jesus or to evangelise the world. Reading the Holy Bible with understanding, translating faith into action and establishing good relationship with God is a good practice in spiritual and good morality. To do what God wants us to do is to love God as we live in the Kingdom of God here on earth. To be believers in God is to be the citizens of His Kingdom which is necessary. Paul's advice to all believers in God through Jesus Christ, for them to be effective in the world as Jesus' apostles, is in (**Romans 12:1–2**): *"Therefore, I urge you, brothers and sisters, in view of God's mercy, to offer your bodies as a living sacrifice holy and pleasing to God. This is your true and proper worship. Do not conform to the pattern of this world, but be transformed by the renewing of your mind. Then* *you will be able to test and approve what God's will is, his good, pleasing and perfect will."*

Those who are called by God should not strive for self-realisation in light of God only but also for the consideration of other people as true images of God whom He loves as well. Seeking the lost to experience the other side of life, is of a vital importance for the transformation of the world. To help people live well on earth, with hope to perpetuate their lives eternally through faith in Jesus Christ and by God's grace, should be aimed at. Time to serve the Lord diligently and effectively, is when the body and soul are still intact. Worshipping the Lord, celebrations and eternal peace will be the experiences of the saved ones.

If anyone feels called by God, let them not delay to join the holy war against the devil by having the spiritual exercises of studying the Bible with understanding, praying ceaselessly, putting into practice their faith in the invincible Creator of heaven and earth. There should be no compromise with sin in thought, word and deed. If the universal church disintegrates in its mission to win souls for Jesus Christ, sin will multiply and overwhelm the people of God who were supposed to inherit the Kingdom of God. It takes faith, courage and perseverance to win battles against the evil forces that are around and keep on haunting people in the world. Some believers fall into apostasy to save their lives and abandon serving God and the people.

History repeats itself. What once happened in the Roman Empire during the reign of the emperor Domitian, in AD 81 – 96 can happen in our days in any part of the world because the invisible evil powers can invade some people, especially those in power to oppress or ill-treat the citizens in any nation to the extent of exterminating them in the power struggle. The corrupt minds are dangerous in any society for they are unpredictable. the devil makes the dependable, undependable to the frustration and detriment of people in the society, making it hard for them to rise above culture to do the will of God. The will of God, will always be reminding us of our evil intentions and practices that offend Him. Love, self-control, patience and endurance should be upheld as the moral virtues in doing the work of the Lord. Those who become power hungry resort to the law of the jungle – the survival of the fittest. They disregard God's ownership of the world to whom they are accountable for their deeds.

The churches as the army of God against sin should unite and speak with one voice against any social evils that dehumanise people to the status of animals. Some of the people who behave like gods do not observe the dignity of human life and this raises the anger of God which might be manifested in the form of calamities like what happened during the Old Testament time. In the Bible, it is stated that God got angry at human violence. He got angry at powerful leaders who oppressed other human beings. The thing that made God angrier than anything else in the Bible was Israel's constant covenant betrayal. Those things that happened in the Bible are happening even today when the powerful rebel against their Creator by disobeying His rule that calls for justice and righteousness among His people (AMOS 5:9-24). God spoke to the people of the northern Kingdom of Israel and He still speaks to the people of today because He is immutable in His love and fulfilment of his promises to remain faithful to Himself.

Does the God of the Bible get angry? Yes, He does because He hates sins though He loves the perpetrators and give them a period of grace to repent. If people refuse to repent, there are serious consequences that follow their deeds on earth and in heaven. The Bible shows that God can get angry with the disobedient people as the following texts state:(DEUTERONOMY 9:8, EXODUS 15:7, EXODUS 32:10 -11, NUMBERS 11:1-2, JOB 4:9, ISAIAH 13:5, JEREMIAH 32:29, LAMENTATION 2:2, NUMBERS 32:13, 2 KINGS 13:3, ISAIAH 51:10, EZEKIEL 7:8, HABAKKUK 3:12, ISAIAH 13:9, MATTHEW 21:12-13, MATTHEW 3:7, PSALMS 78:59), what God was, is and forever will be. He is merciful and slow to anger as is stated in PSALM 86:15, *"But you, Lord are a compassionate and gracious God, slow to anger, abounding in love and faithfulness."* If God was quick to anger and merciless who would be breathing on earth as sinful as we are? His love, patience and mercy should not be regarded as the weakness of God but his immutability in His love and holiness. Because God is patient, He gives His people time to examine themselves and repent from their sins that is why He delays to destroy the world because of its sinfulness as stated in **Ezekiel 33 :11**, say to them, *"As surely as I live, declares the Sovereign Lord, I take no pleasure in the death of the wicked but rather that they turn from their ways and live".* Turn! Turn from your evil ways! Why will you die people of Israel?" These words are said to us all today, God wants us to repent before death strikes. We live long and accumulate wealth without repenting to our own peril, for we will not live forever here on earth. Wise people become penitent before death visits them. Believers in God through Jesus, hope to meet Jesus face to face as it is expressed in the hymn "***Face to face with Christ my Savior.***"

[1] Face to face with Christ, my Savior,
Face to face what will it be,
When with rapture I behold him,
Jesus Christ who died for me?

Chorus

Face to face shall I behold him,
Far beyond the starry sky,
Face to face in all his glory,
I shall see him by and by!

[2] Only faintly now I see him,
With the darkening Veil between,
But a blessed day is coming,
When his glory shall be seen,

[3] What rejoicing in his presence,
When are banished grief and pain;
When the crooked ways are straightened,
And the dark things shall be plain.

[4] Face to face! Oh, blissful moment!
Face to face to see and know
Face to face with my Redeemer
Jesus Christ who loves me so.

Victory is certain for believers in Jesus Christ because He has already won victory through His death and resurrection. Our faith in Jesus, the specific revelation of God to humanity coupled with God's grace will result to our salvation that leads to eternity (John 3 :16).

When we rise above culture, we will be shown the things that we had not known before by the almighty God as He stated in the book of (Jeremiah 33:3), "Call to me and I will answer you and tell you great and unsearchable things you do not know. If we remove doubt from our minds concerning God's revelation to us, the way to salvation becomes clear to see and we will be able to sing joyfully the war hymn: **"Onward Christian Soldiers"**.

> [1] Onward Christian soldiers!
> Marching as to war,
> With the cross of Jesus
> Going on before.
> Christ, the royal master,
> Leads against the foe,
> Forward into battle,
> See, his banner go!
>
> *Chorus*
>
> Onward Christian soldiers!
> Marching as to war,
> With the cross of Jesus,
> Going on before.
>
> [2] At the name of Jesus
> Satan's host doth flee,
> On then, Christian soldiers, onto victory!
> Hell's foundations quiver
> At the shout of praise;
> Brothers, lift your voices,
> Loud your anthems raise,

³ Like a mighty army
Moves the Church of God,
Brothers, we are treading
Where the Saints have trod
We are not divided, all one body we;
One in faith and doctrine,
One eternally,

⁴ Crowns and Thrones may perish,
Kingdoms rise and wane,
But the Church of Jesus
Constant will remain.
Gates of hell can never
against the church prevail,
we have Christ on promise, which can never fail.

⁵ Onward, then ye people!
Join our happy throng
Blend with ours your voices
In the triumph song.
Glory, loud and honor unto Christ, the king,
This through countless ages
Men and angels sing.

Giving hope to lone parents

Human beings as God stewards, should care for the created creatures. There are times when human beings themselves who are stewards need care in the society for them to function well. The natural principle of interdependence should be upheld to alleviate some social problems that some of the people face. The churches especially, should be seen to have the concern for lone parents. Ministries should be formed to care for those in need of assistance.

Those churches that have social concerns ministries should see that the lone parents are included in their objectives to be fulfilled annually. When the family is intact as husband and wife, social and economic problems can be solved comfortably well by using collective ideas for existence. When one of the two is absent owing to death or divorce situations caused are synonymous. Viable or stable work, food, shelter, clothes, education, healthcare, childcare and advice demand constant attention. The parent meetings should be organised where lone parents can come together to share their problems. It is in such interactions that possible solutions can be found. Counsellors, ministers of religion, social workers and educationists can be invited to these meetings to give some lectures on the topics suggested by the lone parents themselves. Such meetings can boost the lone parents' confidence in their family care and get rid of stress or depression.

It is advisable for the churches to have some recreation centres where people can meet for different social activities and arranged group discussions or studies. Fellowship that is missing in the one parent family can be found in groups. It is in these groups that the young lone parents can discuss the possibilities to remarry after seriously studying the advantages and disadvantages of remarriage. Paul gives advice on single parents in **1 Corinthians 7:8–9**. Lone parenting of children is not a new social phenomenon, but its disadvantages need to be curbed by possible solutions like group work of the single parents in the neighbourhood by giving each other some responsibilities to carry out, at a given time to have enough time to fend for the families.

Help in caring for children can be sourced even from the two parent families who may volunteer to give help at the planned times. Parents should be open minded to their fellowship groups so that some of the people in or outside the fellowship can give the needed assistance. Human beings are social beings as they live among other people. This is the plan of God, so that the needy can be assisted as God Himself assists humanity.

Charitable groups should be formed to care for those in need of help materially. The Chisipiti High School in Zimbabwe, has a motto in Latin that reads thus: "Fons vitae caritas," meaning the fountain or source of life is charity or love. Where there is no love, life becomes very difficult. Scholarships for short courses, can make the willing students acquire some of the needed skills that can be helpful in life. This is food for thought in lone parents' fellowship. The adage, "Necessity is the mother of invention" should be taken seriously in social groups.

It is generally felt that self-discipline as lone parents, is necessary in preparation for remarriage. The writer, when he was in active ministry as an ordained minister of the United Methodist Church, used to attend the lone parents' fellowships. Very helpful lessons used to be delivered and some of these lone parents were married and they are happily living in their homes. God has good plans for us all. To show that God cared for his people in the Babylonian captivity, He had this to say to them when time for their liberation from captivity was approaching, *"For I know the plans I have for you, declares the Lord, plans to prosper you and not to harm you, plans to give you hope and a future"* (JEREMIAH 29:11).

Those who choose to remarry will remarry by God's help and those who choose not to remarry but look after the children as lone parents will successfully follow their choice. In both situations, God will give you blessings that will comfort you. Good examples are given in the account about Naomi (RUTH 1:3–22) a prophetess Anna (LUKE 2:36–38). God's blessings can come in different ways to comfort us in our loneliness. Children in families can grow up well, have good education and employment. Their children can have the drive to strengthen the families socially, economically and spiritually. As a lone parent the mother of the late president of Zimbabwe was able to raise his son who became President Robert Gabriel Mugabe.

The God we worship is the God of history who is involved in all our social activities. In happiness, sorrow and other situations, God is with us to guide and protect us. We always say that we feel lonely in the absence of life partners, parents and friends. These are the people who can be seen but the invisible Almighty God is among us whom we call "Pfuyanherera" in Shona language spoken in Zimbabwe which means, "one who cares for orphans." Those who rise above culture feel for others and act sacrificially to witness their welfare in society. Those things which God can do through human beings to others are gracious actions to the needy for their welfare. In the lone parents' fellowship, think-tanks can be formed out of a few people in groups. These people take the responsibility of dreaming dreams as visionaries. They can present types of projects that can be carried out cooperatively for self-reliance like poultry, animal and crop farming for marketing and local consumption. Aiming high in any society is a sign of rising above the culture of indolence, begging, lack of self-esteem and poverty which some people may choose as their way of life to their detriment. Some people might lack the knowledge of running the projects. That is a situation that demands seminars where people who lack equipment, the idea of collective ownership of equipment might find the solution to the problems. Where there are problems, reason can capture ideas from the metaphysical world as the Greek philosophers put it, reasoning always yields good results. Those who refuse to reason or find it very difficult or time consuming, cannot be leaders so say some philosophers. The ideas expressed here are for the employed and unemployed lone parents to enhance their self-reliance.

A lone parent who was a school teacher in a rural area school, was approached by a benefactor who would provide her with agricultural inputs like seeds and fertilisers. The idea would assist the lady teacher who had children to care for and send to better schools and she readily accepted the offer. This happened in the year 2020. The teacher cultivated a piece of land planted the crops that happened to be maize, groundnuts and round nuts, using the necessary agricultural inputs. She was surprised to see how the crops grew and so were the local people who had not thought of using this land for a long time. Some of them visited the field and were surprised to see how productive the field was.

Come the harvest time in the year 2021, some people in the locality queued up to be engaged in harvesting the crops. This project did not help this lady teacher alone but others as well in one way or another. The result of diligence motivated the teacher to continue on her own, to till the land near the school and her dwelling place. Tilling the land has become her subculture of having a side-line of income to supplement her meagre salary and now, she is surprisingly swimming with her head above water moneywise. In the year 2021, the same lady planned to raise chickens. Economic development starts small and grows bigger for the good of many if properly managed. This reminds me of the parable of Jesus called: *"The Parable of the mustard seed"* (**Matthew 13:33**). The word of God preached to the people will yield great results in terms of converts. These converts become the citizens of God's kingdom on earth and multiply in number as they develop spiritually and morally. Aiming high is always a thing we ought to do at school, home, and places of employment, spiritually and morally to rise above a retrogressive culture with customs which are anti progress, anti–social and apathetic. The adage "Nothing venture, nothing have" is irrefutable in life.

It takes one or a few people to initiate the reawakening of human minds to be industrious. If the ideas of social industrialisation are grasped in any society, people rise above the oppressive culture to fight against hunger, poverty, diseases and unemployment. We need money in solving most of our social problems in the world. When we defeat these problems, the crime rate will follow to the same fate. It is ideal for governments to equip people with knowledge to be able to navigate in the world full of challenges. Governments should think seriously about free education from year one to the high school education to help parents keep money for their children's further education. The government should also think of having some bursaries for the able students to do their university work. To join the government in this venture are some business people whose businesses will not be affected adversely by setting aside a few dollars from their profits for charity. To rise above culture is to think about other people in need so that we all progress rather than laughing at them. Help others to rise above low social strata by empowering them educationally and economically. This may sound to be impossible and yet the Holy Bible, the word of God, approves it. What God tells us to do is right to do according to theological ethics.

Doing the will of God, seems to be turning things upside down in adopted customs based on certain norms and values (**Acts 1:5–9**). Doing the right things is misconstrued as acting wrongly by those who may be involved in exploiting others and involved in corruption to enrich themselves. Where is righteousness and justice in such practices in light of God? Practices that are against the will of God, even if they take us to their climax of our joy, should be abandoned. To seek to please ourselves against the will of God and to the disadvantage of others with whom we cohabit on earth is a sin. That tastes like a bitter pill to some and yet taking a bitter pill, can be a cure for the ailment one is suffering from. We should not forget that God's judgement at the end of the known time is based on our present attitudes and behaviour towards God's will.

It is not a thing to boast about for an exploiter to enjoy life excessively at the expense of the exploited people living in agony in their dwelling places. Social bad practices take toll on human lives in our sight, and we pretend we see nothing and so we cannot say anything. Talking about things at home, social institutions and parliament can enlighten some hard-hearted people to think about changing their attitudes and behaviour for the good of all. Silence affects people negatively as they get into the mental process of slow development that ends up in having dead conscience. We should not forget that Jesus came into the world to liberate us from different types of bondages. It is prudent for us to do what God would like us to do (**LUKE 4:18**).

Some governments that have risen above culture, take care of the needy, aged, physically and mentally incapacitated whereas others who are inconsiderate, leave the problems to families themselves. When we rule, we rule on behalf of the Sovereign God who cares for all people irrespective of their status in life. All people have the right to live. The dignity of life is a virtue to be observed. The welfare of people is to be budgeted for very carefully. The focus of any government should be people when plans are made for education, farming, health, transport, mining and welfare. Such activities should be for the good and welfare of the citizens and those outside the government's jurisdiction (**PSALM 68:5; PSALM 10:14; DEUTERONOMY 10:18; JAMES 1:27; DEUTERONOMY 14:29; THESSALONIANS 5:24**). If we become addicted to the ways we do things when they are wrong, it becomes a social anomaly to do. New wine cannot be kept in the old wineskin that has reached the end of its electricity for when the wine reaches the stage of fermentation it will burst. Then new wine should be kept in the new wine skin as said by Jesus in His parable of the wine skins (**Matthew 9:14 to 17**; **Mark 2:18–22**; **Luke 5:33–39**). Those who have the capacity to take new teachings because of their positive attitudes will accommodate the new teachings. Those who are full of "I know" attitudes, like the old wineskins, will not contain the new progressive teachings because of their habitual attitude of negativity. The Lord says to those who are hard hearted, *"I will give you a new heart and put a new spirit in you; I will remove from you your heart of stone and give you a heart of flesh. And I will put my spirit in you and move you to follow my decrees and be careful to keep my laws. Then you live in the land I gave your ancestors; you will be my people and I will be your God"* (**Ezekiel 36:26–28**).

When God speaks, we should all listen and respond positively because God, our Lord is holy and He wants what He says to be followed righteously and justly by people created in His image. The way we live will differ from the way we ought to live on earth if the will of God is not followed. We must try our best to please God as we live together on earth.

Carrying a tin with holes at the bottom to fetch water, from the well repeatedly without noticing the leakage, is a sign of insanity. You must sit down and mend that tin to contain water needed for use. At times same people pretend to be insane and shameless, to carry out some evil intentions for self-aggrandisement or to fulfil some corrupt intentions. One of God's names is "El Roi" – God who sees me. Nothing is hidden from Him and even our thoughts are clear to Him.

"With men this is impossible but with God all things are possible" (Matthew 19:26)

Jesus Christ, the son of God, when He was teaching his disciples, He noticed that they did not understand what He was teaching them (**Matthew 19:23–26**). To emphasise his teaching, He said, *"With men this is impossible, but with God all things are possible"* (**Matthew 19:26**). A miracle in the holy Bible is called "Miraculum in Latin which is a miracle or a happening that causes wonder and astonishment or unexplainable event by normal standards. The God we worship is the God of miracles. What is impossible is possible through the power of God who created things "exnihilo"– out of nothing. Empowered by God, the followers of Jesus performed miracles in healing and exorcism in the New Testament even during our time miracles happen through faith. Faith in God through Jesus, helps people to rise above the normal situations which are at human level. The supernatural happenings in our realm, indicate the presence of the invisible God who makes the impossible possible. In Isaiah **43:19** God said, *"See I am doing a new thing! Now it springs up; do you not perceive it? I am making a way in the wilderness and streams in the Wasteland."* God is at work in human history to provide air we breathe in, water we drink, light, food, shelter, guidance and protection. It is God who helps people to be liberated from ailments, oppression of any kind so that people can enjoy freedom and safety under His rule on earth.

God brings about liberation and true peace of mind which supersedes all understanding.

Through faith in God perseverance and innovation, human beings can do many wonderful things for the good of humanity. This is why we should always aim high to do better spiritually, scientifically, economically and politically as God's stewards on earth. Refusing to improve in our ways of living and ruling people is a serious sign of negligence of our responsibilities on earth. At times we blame God for our own mistakes. When God provides us with groundnuts, we should not expect Him to shell the nuts and feed us. God has already given us the ability to do things within the range of human possibility.

All things that make life possible on the planet have been provided by God. All we have to do is to use our minds to reason out what we ought to do for survival. Through some social interactions, we can know some of the things to be done for our existence on earth. Churches, Schools, colleges, universities and hospitals can contribute a lot of ideas on how to live safely on the planet. Ignorance, doubting, lack of courage in the life of people, are like hurdles to jump to reach the truth that liberates from different challenges. Through ignorance, unbelief or doubt, things seem so far and yet so near; so impossible and yet possible. The insurmountable are surmountable with God's assistance for our knowledge and power are naturally limited.

The letter of Paul to the **PHILIPPINES 4:13** Paul says, *"I can do all this through him who gives me strength."* This means that no matter what circumstances I face, I can respond with the strength of Christ who strengthens me. All inventions were made out of necessity. To rise above culture, we should feel the passion to invent new things so as to meet our needs. Practical subjects like agriculture, economics, animal farming, science, religion, sociology, technology, building and carpentry should be taught in schools to equip people to deal with challenges in life. For our economy, the primary source is the land. The soil and the minerals underneath it, can meet most of the needs of the people, if handled responsibly to raise the standard of living of the people. If God orders us to do certain things, they can be done according to his plan, to fulfil definite purposes.

In the face of challenges, God provides with outlets or solutions by His grace. What God does amongst us draws us close to Him like what the fish and other domesticated animals do when you provide them with food. The giving and receiving interaction between God and people is met with people's reciprocation in honour and worship. God is the ground of our existence. We came from Him and on earth, we are in preparation to return to Him for eternal life. No social problems should alienate us from our Maker. Alienation from Him invites eternal death as what Paul says in his letter to the **ROMANS 8:35–39**. Living In need or abundance, God is God who should be worshipped eternally for what He is. The prophet Habakkuk's Experiences of God be treated as shared experiences with us also. He said in his prayer to God, *"Lord I have heard of your fame; I stand in awe of your deeds, Lord. Repeat them in our day, in our time make them known; in wrath remember mercy"* (**HABAKKUK 3:2**). Our attitude towards God should be like that of Habakkuk who said, *"Though the fig tree does not bud and there are no grapes on the vines, though the olive crop fails and the fields produce no food, though there are no sheep in the pen and no cattle* *in the stalls, Yet I will rejoice in the Lord, I will be joyful in God my saviour"* (**HABAKKUK 3:17–18**). Through social problems Satan tries hard to dampen our faith in God. If we resist him, he will flee. The Lord promised the people in the past and still promises us today about our future till the end of time. We have been told by the Lord what to do when we are bombarded by needs or surrounded by problems in his sermon on the mount in **MATTHEW 7:7–8**, *"Ask and it will be given to you; Seek and you will find; Knock and the door will be opened to you. For everyone who asks receives, the one who seeks finds; and to one who knocks the door will be opened."* This reminds the writer of a song titled, **"Whisper A Prayer."**

> [1] Whisper a prayer in the morning,
> Whisper a prayer at noon,
> Whisper a prayer in the evening,
> To keep your heart in tune.
>
> [2] God answers prayer in the morning,
> God answers prayer at noon,
> God answers prayer in the evening,
> To keep your heart in tune.
>
> [3] Jesus may come in the morning,
> Jesus may come at noon,
> Jesus may come in the evening,
> So keep your heart in tune.

When we dialogue with God, He listens and answers all prayers sooner or later according to His will. Jesus is like a very clean mirror. When we stand before a mirror, we see ourselves clearly. We see what we need to correct about ourselves in appearance and correct what is unsightly before we stand before the public. Jesus goes further to reveal what can corrupt the inner self before it corrupts others so that we correct it. To rise above culture, we need someone extraordinary to occupy our hearts and minds, so as to be impervious to corruption and be philanthropic in character. We need day by day sanctification by the Holy Spirit till death to be acceptable in the sight of God.

Although there are so many things that we ought to do as people who sin daily against God in thought, word, deed and through omission, we still need to hunger after righteousness. God is pleased with such people because He quickly comes to their aid to meet their needs. For one to be a conqueror spiritually one has to wrestle with the devil and defeat him. On our own we cannot conquer him because we are body and soul whereas the devil is an invisible spirit. To defeat the devil, we need the assistance of the Triune God who is invisible and almighty "Deus Semper Invictus Est" – God is always invincible. His joy is our strength as is said in **NEHEMIAH 8:10**, *"Enjoy choice food and sweet drinks, and send some to those who have nothing prepared this is holy to our Lord. Do not grieve, for the joy of the Lord is your strength."* To do good is to please God and to please God is to ask for the blessing of strength to continue to do good in the society. As people who have been raised above culture by God, to do good of every kind is expected of us by the Lord. Doing good is the nature of God that can be found in a believer and an unbeliever although the latter might not realise it. Anything evil done by a believer or an unbeliever emanates from the devil for the devil is incapable of doing anything good.

Any believer who endeavours to live a righteous life is in right relationship with God. Consequently, they become frequent messengers of God involved in evangelising others in the society and their character is expected to be unquestionable. As a result of their character, they are trusted in their responsibilities by those with whom they live. God enables them to do great works as instruments for salvation. God works directly with all the people or through people whom he chooses either believers or unbelievers. It is the purpose for which they are chosen that needs to be done. God gives authority to achieve His purpose in the world. It is the state of one's election by God that elevates one to function effectively in the work that is to be done. The Bible abounds with many characters who were enabled to do great works by God. What God did then, is what he does even today. Those who are called or chosen should humble themselves before God and the people as it is sung in the hymn **"Have Thine Own Way, Lord."**

[1] Have thine own way Lord
Have thine own way
Thou art the Potter I am the clay
Mould me and make me after Thy will
While I am waiting yielded and still

[2] Have Thine own way Lord
Have Thine own way
Search me and try me Master today
Whiter than snow Lord wash me just know
As in Thy presence humbly I bow

[3] Have Thine own way Lord
Have Thine own way
Hold over my being absolute away
Filled with thy spirit till all can see
Christ only always living in me

Disobedience of the chosen people leads to their abandonment by God and the power given to them is withdrawn. Faithfulness in the performance of God's work is of vital importance. The chosen should dedicate and rededicate themselves to the almighty God to be connected to the source of power, and wisdom in the earthly life.

Hymns, gospel songs and choruses in the life of a Christian believer

Besides studying the Bible, Christian believers have to take a close study of the religious experiences of some of them when they had an encounter with God. The composers or singers express their Christian theological experiences in poems and songs when they meet God in their lives. Some of their experiences are in the hymn books, song books and others are unwritten but expressed orally.

Even if we cannot sing or sing well these hymns, songs or choruses because we do not know them or have not learnt them, we should take time to read and understand their meanings. We will be surprised how deep they are in their theological interpretations of the composers. In the end, we might seek to learn how to sing their songs so that we enjoy the shared experiential theology expressed in the songs. We might find out some similarities in experiences between the present and the church before us who are our forerunners in the Christian faith. These hymns and songs will encourage us today to continue to run the race in faith as the forerunners did. Such an attitude will help us to be courageous or more courageous in that some of the forerunners did not abandon their faith till death. We need to be mature in faith for us to be able to show the new converts the way to salvation. We should guard against secular practices that try to or infiltrate the church to destabilise it.

Church discipline should be adhered to, to create good systems to carry out church activities. Practising church activities with ulterior motives will always be misleading and will retard the growth of the Church. Those who come to church genuinely are trying hard to run away from sin and the anger of God. It is in the church where they can have a sanctuary spiritually and psychologically. The church is not a place where secular activities also thrive because they will contaminate the sacred things that need to be taken spiritually and psychologically. To rise above culture, one who is called should have a discerning spirit to quickly differentiate good practices from the bad ones for the church to run well anywhere in the world to serve its purpose.

Churches are mushrooming. Some of them with very weak backgrounds misleading unsuspicious followers. Some of them concentrate on social gospel that focuses on wealth and little teaching on genuine repentance for the forgiveness of sins like what the biblical preachers did. Wealth should be gained faithfully without any deceitful means. Christians should find good ways of making money rather than fanatically seeding money in persons. Proper charity to help the needy is acceptable because this was the practice of the early church that has become the tradition of the church to this time. The old church is to be in existence today because God works through disciplined believers who are serious about ecclesiastical goals. The church is first and foremost, an institution of salvation. Works of love are taught by our Lord in the parable of the Good Samaritan, as acts of faith for the church to avoid the spiritual dichotomy of faith whereby Christians are tempted to cling to the affirmation of belief devoid of works (JAMES 2:14–26).

The traditional churches should stick to the church tradition as they work meticulously trying to take in some practices from other sources. The borrowed practices should be there only to strengthen the church rather than to demotivate believers. Adopted practices should be the result of serious church consensus in properly organised meetings. This helps the worshippers to worship with clear conscience in fear of God. Martin Luther's words, "Sola Scriptura"– "Scriptures Only," should be adhered to in church practices because the scriptures or the Holy Bible is the revelation of God to humanity. The writer strongly feels this is the way to rise above culture in our social and religious activities. Remember the warning given to the church by the apostle Peter to the church in the past and present, *"Be alert and of sober mind. Your enemy the devil prowls around like a roaring lion looking for someone to devour. Resist him, standing firm in the faith, because you know that the family of believers throughout the world is undergoing the same kind of sufferings"* (1 PETER 5:8–9).

Many believers have suffered and even died for being apologists of the faith. Because of their daring stand, the church is here today. The church will go on till Jesus comes to the earth visibly at the end of time. Those who make up the church are the chosen few and the body of our Lord Jesus. Because Jesus Christ is alive, the church is the active body of Christ continuing with the mission of Jesus on earth (LUKE 4:18–19).

We can defend our faith, but we cannot defend God because He is eternally invincible. Our faith that is composed of doctrines can be tampered with by some of philosophical believers to sound real and yet destructive and misleading. Did Jesus Christ not warn His disciples to watch and pray? Are we not also Jesus' disciples and apostles? Watch and pray! *"Watch and pray so that you will not fall into temptation." The spirit is willing but the flesh is weak,"* Jesus said (MATTHEW 26:41).

Paul in a second letter to Timothy had this as a warning to Timothy, *"But mark this there will be terrible times in the last days. People will be lovers of themselves, lovers of money, boastful, proud, abusive, disobedient to their parents, ungrateful, and unholy, without love, unforgiving, slanderous, without self–control, brutal, nor lovers of the good, treacherous, rash, lovers of pleasure rather than lovers of God, conceited, lovers of pleasure rather than lovers of God – having a form of godliness but denying its power. Have nothing to do with such people"* (**2 Timothy 3:1–5**). Are we not living in that time today? Are we yet to see these happenings taking place in the near or remote future? God is omniscient, He knows where we are now but we, human beings, with the limited minds we have remained undecided. The church is in the accompaniment of its owner, Jesus Christ, Himself till the end of time. Clinging to our faith till death while fighting against sin is the attitude to adopt as we rise above culture. Our forefathers in faith, sang a hymn titled "***The Church is One Foundation.***"

[1] The churches one foundation
Is Jesus Christ her Lord;
She is his new creation
By water and the word:
From heaven he came and sought her
To be his holy bride;
With his own blood he bought her,
And for her life he died.

[2] Elect from every nation,
Yet one over all the earth;
Her charter of salvation.
One Lord, one faith, one birth:
One holy name she blesses,
Partakes one holy food;
To one hope she presses,
With every grace endued.

3 The church will never perish,
Her dear Lord to defend,
To guide, sustain and cherish, is with her till the end.
Tho' there be those that hate her fail,
Against both foe and traitor she ever shall prevail.

4 Tho' with a scornful wonder
The world sees her apprehend,
By schism rent asunder,
By heresies distressed,
Yet Saints their watch are keeping,
Their cry goes up" How long? "
And soon the night of weeping
Shall be the morn of song.

5 'Mid toil and tribulation
And tumult of her war
She waits the consummation of peace forevermore
All the vision glorious
Her longing eyes are blest,
And the church victorious
Shall be the church at rest.

Oh, how inspiring this hymn authored by S.J stone (1866) to give the descendants spiritual wealth and food for life journey until we reach home! Hallelujah, Jesus is accompanying the church to its destination despite tribulations! A hymn like this one, gives courage to the believer to soldier on against all odds in the life journey for the great reward that no person can give on earth but the Creator which is eternal life.

The significance of hymns and Christian songs

It is generally believed that the church hymns serve as a prayer of Thanksgiving and an expression of commitment. Many hymns build unity among believers as well as build a community of believers. These hymns invite the Holy Spirit into meetings and our lives.

Hymns are God centred and call our attention upward during the "Kairos" time – the special time of communicating with God, the Sovereign Ruler and our Owner. The worshippers are drawn to a higher level of spiritual experience different from the physical experience in the "Chronos" time, the ordinary time in the daily life when secular things are the object of our search.

The hymns synchronised the church denominational doctrines that reveal the church's oneness despite the different names they bear. The church, is one. It is referred to as the Catholic or universal church whose Head is Jesus. The church is like a big family made up of many children with different talents, ages and views. The differences of the family members do not make the unity of church oblivious or truly physically absent. This is what we call unity in diversity with mutual respect. The God who called the members of the denomination, is the same God who called the members of the other denominations. The members of the denominations can move from one denomination to another of their spiritual persuasion according to their personal convictions. The focus of the Catholic Church is the Triune God whose Universality is the common experience to all the denominations. Some of the hymns show us how the "original sin" and the sins we commit are overcome through faith in Jesus Christ. That theological concept is based on biblical teachings so we can uphold our faith and hope in our spiritual journey.

It is generally believed that teams of believers can give children a solid foundation in Christian doctrines. They can help children to understand the Bible better. The common experience generated by hymns in individual or corporate worship is energisation of faith or importation of courage to face even the fierce situations. Worshippers, at times, sing about biblical characters who held unwavering faith and courage like Noah, Abraham, Isaac, Joseph, David, Shadrack, Misheck, Abednego and Daniel, the prophets and apostles who suffered because of preaching about Jesus at the expense of their lives. James even died a martyr in prison because of his faith in Jesus. Peter, Paul and Silas were thrown into prison with some physical torture. Sacrificial faith is introduced in following Jesus. Rising above culture takes some sacrifices.

Hymns are complementary to biblical studies for the achievement of common purpose. King David in the Bible, is known as a famous singer who expressed his theology in poems and songs. The hymns of the same essence throughout the ages play a very important role in worship and evangelization of the people in the world. Some songs and choruses are composed by the current singers from their current experiences and from biblical perspectives. Believers and non-believers are motivated by these songs and choruses. Some churches or denominations, have the custom of writing songs and choruses in the form of books which is a good practice. Those who sing songs and choruses by rote memory should adopt the system of writing down these songs and choruses for the benefit of their successors in faith. Tradition has it that the teachings and church practices should be handed over to the followers for continuity of doctrines and phenomenological religious experiences for practical theology in Worship.

What was in the past, is in the present and future in relation to things that trouble human beings in life. These things make them restless and cause ailments. They affect the body, soul and mind. One who can deal with these problems is none other than Jesus who was originally known as "The Word" who, through the incarnation on earth, came to be known as Jesus. When surrounded by all life-threatening problems people are urged to hum or sing the comforting hymn like, "**What A Friend We Have In Jesus.**"

> [1] What a friend we have in Jesus
> All our sins and griefs to bear!
> What a privilege to carry
> Everything God in prayer!
>
> *Chorus*
>
> O what peace we often forfeit,
> Oh, what needless pain we bear,
> All because we do not carry
> Everything to God in prayer!

² Have we trials and temptations?
Is there trouble anywhere?
We should never be discouraged;
Take it to the Lord in prayer!
Can we find a friend so faithful?
Who will all our sorrows share?
Jesus knows all every weakness;
Take it to the Lord in prayer!

³ Are we weak and heavy laden,
Cumbered with a load of care?
Precious Saviour, still our refuge–
Take it to the Lord in prayer!
Do your friends despise, forsake you?
Take it to the Lord in prayer!
In his arms he'll take and shield you;
You will find a solace there.

There are troubles or problems of different kinds in the families, societies and workplaces and at times, even in the church that cannot be solved by parents, social workers or parliamentarians, human resources personnel and in the church, by the fellow believers or the pastors. We are urged by the hymn "What a friend we have in Jesus" to take these problems to God in prayer. God will solve the problems in His own way. It can be through inspiring individuals to do some counselling, healing or by directly transforming the minds of the individuals who cause problems. The greatest liberator from all types of bondages on earth is God, our Creator who is one with His Son, Jesus and the Holy Spirit. The God we worship is invincible He gives us comfort and hope for our salvation. This hymn is sung mostly in times of bereavement and when calamity strikes, the one who knows no defeat, Jesus, is in control of all situations. When He was physically on earth, he silenced the storm, healed the sick, fed the hungry, consoled the bereaved and raised the dead. This shows us that God is very concerned with human beings. Jesus still lives but, in the spirit, like God the Father. He is everywhere. According to the letter to the **HEBREWS 13:8**, we are told clearly about the eternal presence and immutability of Jesus for us not to doubt. The verse says, *"Jesus Christ is the same yesterday and today and forever."* Let's confide in God always for He will fight battles for us. What He promises, He fulfils. There are times when people blame God for their inadequacy materially, when they have been endowed with some talents they can utilise for their good. People cannot all be rich but we can, at least, have our daily bread although physical and mental incapacities can be challenges that can hamper our effectiveness to do some work. At times, unemployment in urban areas can make people desperate but most of the people in the rural areas are self–employed and able to provide themselves with the necessities of life. God provides us with means of survival during the difficult times. Paul once spoke about experiencing times of want and times of need but with the help of Jesus he was able to accommodate the situations. Paul said in his letter to the Philippines 4:11–13, *"I am not saying this because I am in need, for I have learned to be content whatever the circumstances. I know what it is to be in need, and I know what it is to have plenty. I have learned the secret of being content in any and every situation whether well fed or hungry, whether living in plenty or in want. I can do all this through him who gives me strength."* All life situations we meet today in our lives, are not new for they have been experienced by others before. Let's find out how they overcame. Accumulate the knowledge to succeed from the wise and add it to yours to enable you to rise Above culture in order to see what is right or wrong, good or bad in any culture.

We worship the impartial God that is why He loves all the people, though He hates the sinful activities they do. We are what God chose us to be naturally. However, because of our attitudes and behaviour we are not what we ought to be. Let us change what we can change about ourselves and leave to God what is not in our knowledge and power to change. We should not look down upon ourselves for conditions that are natural or created for us by others. We should feel sorry with ourselves for failing to change changeable conditions we have created for ourselves. We should not blame God for our own mistakes or other people. Let's not look for scapegoats for what we do or happens to ourselves when we know we are the cause. All we need to do is to repent.

The Hymn Count your blessings will help us see the good things God does for us which are not even acknowledged with gratitude. We depend on the very important gifts of God for our existence and yet we cease to worship God because of certain gifts we expect to have. Let's praise God first and foremost, that we are living for without life all these other things we have or want to possess are useless. Who will use them if we are not there and yet we had meant them to be used by us? Let us open our eyes and minds to notice the good things that God has provided us. The composer of the hymn "***Count Your Blessings***," has this to say to all the people to stop blaming God for lack of small things we can even manage to go without!

[1] When upon life's billows you are Tempest tossed,
When you're discouraged all is lost,
Count your many blessings, name them one by one,
And it will surprise you what the Lord hath done.

Refrain

Count your blessings, name them one by one;
Count your blessings, see what God hath done,
Count your blessings, name them one by one,
Count blessings, see what God hath done.

[2] Are you burdened with a load of care?
Does the cross seem heavy you are called to bear?
Count your many blessings; ev'ry doubt will fly.
And you'll be singing as days go by.

[3] When you look at others with their lands and gold,
Think that Christ has promised you his wealth untold;
Count your many blessings, money cannot buy
Your reward in heaven, not your home on high.

[4] So amid the conflict, whether great or small,
Do not be discouraged, God is overall;
Count your many blessings, angels will attend,
Help comfort give you to your journey's end.

Baptist hymnal 1991.

This hymn helps the singers' and the listeners' state of hopelessness with God's help. Those who sing and listen will feel uplifted spiritually and continue to soldier on in all life situations. This hymn is like the song of a great singer in the Bible – King David's song is popularly recited and sung today in worship during times of bereavement. **PSALM 23:1–6**, helped King David to gather courage and profound faith in God to carry out his responsibilities against all odds to God's satisfaction and pleasure. We should learn from the successful ones to do well or better in life with the help of God.

David, in his song, made his commitment to dwell in the house of God forever. The House of the Lord is a place of safety spiritually, mentally and physically. It is God who is ever with us to guide and protect us. Fear is distanced by courage when we confide in God. When a person is attacked physically or dies while holding faith in God, the life remains secure in the hands of God as they euphemistically, lie asleep awaiting the resurrection. Life continues in eternity for true believers in God.

During the period when the body and soul are still intact, the period of grace, is the time to prepare for eternity in heaven through obedience to God and trying our best to live a righteous or clean life before God and people with whom we live on earth. It is only when we fight courageously against temptations and sins that victory in Jesus Christ can be experienced or witnessed. There cannot be any victory if there is not any battle fought through faith in God. Wise parents work hard to train their children to be brave fighters by training them when they are still young to have faith in God for them to be connected to the source of wisdom and power to conquer the devil as they live on earth. Education for living, is necessary in all developmental stages of a child to adulthood. Failure to impart such education is a great deal of disservice to children. In the Holy Bible, the book of **PROVERBS 22:1–16** is indeed, an appropriate text and good food for the mind and soul in bringing up children to be responsible people in the society. **PROVERBS 22:6** is a very important advice to the parents in nurturing children. Elder Jack H. Goaslind once said, "I believe most parents try to teach their children right from wrong to be honest, to respect others and their property, to live morally, clean lives, and to love their Families."

Everyone has the potential to do good or bad. Doing good or bad goes by practice and persistence. Constant practice becomes a norm or character of an individual in the Society. When one is in the habit to use their mind to lie, they become liars. When their interest is inclined to telling the truth, they become honest in life. Liars become enemies of fellow people because they are unreliable and misleading. Those who tell the truth become dependable or persons of integrity and good leaders in the society.

The young adults can be liars or honest depending on how they grow up or are brought up. Heredity and environment influence roles to play in good and bad people. Selfishness, pride, grudges, hatred and fear are rife in liars whereas love, kindness, courage and peace often influence the attitude of the honest individuals who tend to be loved, respected and even chosen to be leaders in the society. Liars, can deceitfully become leaders also unfortunately because of their lies, anger and cruelty. People of like mind, go for them with ulterior motives to destroy, to promote their relatives and oppress those who are not of their tribal or racial group. Those who rise above culture choose to imitate God who loves all people whom He created in His image. Talents or abilities are suppressed by certain unreliable individuals to the extent of retarding development and prosperity in any society. Their own adherence to God's specific revelation, is the answer for them to see clearer what ought to be done to rise above retrogressive and oppressive culture.

God is love. Love can liberate the oppressor and all the oppressed. In such a situation all people live as free people and have time to plan for their development in the peaceful environment. To be loving, kind and caring, helps to enhance these people's welfare. Where people live in love and upholding caring attitudes, they enjoy mutual respect and, in most cases, they are free from stress or distress and associate ailments. Self–control and empathy become values of the citizens who choose to rise above some bad practices in a culture, in their endeavour to improve themselves in different aspects of life. Good attitudes and behaviour can easily distinguish individuals who practice them to be good persons to live with in the Society. This is to rise above culture in any social group.

Old people would like to be good but when they fail, they become so bad or unbecoming to their detriment. They lose the good name and respect they should have and become wet blankets wherever they happen to find themselves in the society. Turning over a new leaf, is what they need which religiously, is called repentance to be in right relationship with God who is holy and loving.

In education, the basic principle of "readiness" is very significant for anyone to take learning seriously. Without "readiness" no one can learn to change intellectually and spiritually. A person can choose to oppress themselves by inclining to negativity or to liberate themselves by inclining to positivity to good things that bring about development, peace and joy. Choose to do good to rise above culture for the good of all the people.

It seems, in urban areas where both parents are breadwinners, there is very little time for parents to interact with their children who spend most of the time at school. When parents come home from work, they are tired and would like to sleep to rest before they return to work. It is necessary to spend some time with children and talk about life in general. Children themselves should be open to their parents to get the necessary assistance to the problems they may be facing. Children are like seedlings in the nursery that should be given special care before they are transplanted to the permanent beds.

Because of their inexperience, children get into unnecessary social problems, hence adults must always be alert to assist the naive children in dealing with some social problems. Although schools and churches deal with some of the social challenges of the children, parents themselves should play a major role. "Vita magma est" – "Life is great" but short. Careful use of time on earth is of great importance. Social deviance is a waste of the short time in which good and profitable activities need to be done to benefit self, family and the Society. Temperance in luxuries should be applied while diligence should be upheld as personal motto for economic development and self–reliance. Money earned or gained in social enterprises should not be wasted on things one can live without. The adage, "Waste not; want not", should be observed to avert poverty. To help those in need, one is to keep something to handout. It is advisable to leave within one's means. Some people live beyond their means and in the end, they find straining themselves physically and economically. The temptation to compete with anyone whose economic benefit is unknown, can lead to bankruptcy, criminality, suicidal tendencies and even death. Such a competitive ambition should be avoided.

The Holy Bible precisely and clearly admonishes us against covetousness in **Exodus 20:17**, *"You shall not covet your neighbour's house. You shall not covet your neighbour's wife, or his male or female servant, his ox or donkey, or anything that belongs to your neighbour."* Because the Lord has spoken, a person created in His image, "Imago Dei "ought to listen and effect the commandment for their spiritual and ethical uprightness. To do so, is to rise above culture and to live safely in the society. To live according to the will of God, is the primary responsibility of a person.

Making some improvements within one's means is a safe way to take for personal economic development.

Important institutions for enlightenment – churches, universities, colleges and schools

The writer chooses to metaphorically call churches, universities, colleges and the schools as pods of a Munhondo tree (Shona), Umshonkwe (Ndebele), Julbernadia Globiflora (Scientific name) and the tree itself, is metaphorically the Creator who brings things into existence to multiply and fill the earth to fulfil His purpose. What is created by God, pleases Him. Nothing created by God is useless or purposeless. It is God who initiated the concept of having the institutions of socialisation for people's enlightenment for the good of humanity in all aspects of life.

Schools are the elementary growth of pods with the potential of further growth to maturity as are:training colleges, universities and churches.

These pods have seeds like students and members of the church. When they are mature, they are dispersed to different places like seeds are scattered naturally by the pods through explosion. Where these educated or trained people land, becomes the base for the transformation of the environment like the germination of seed dispersed by explosion. The new plants change the land that was even bear. The corporate church brings together the converts and teach them the word of God, to the stage they become full members of the church. Thereafter, they are urged to be involved in church outreach to make the disciples of Jesus. The children who were given informal education by parents at home, are handed over to the institutions where they are given formal education. After the acquisition of the required knowledge and training, the educated or trained individuals, feel confident to face the world and make some contributions in different ways to transform the world. The responsible teachers and religious leaders will help to make the world a better world to live in. The schooled people are supposed to be responsible or dependable to control nature rather than to be controlled by nature. When there's drought they know how to tap water from underground to irrigate fields. When people are ill, they know how the ailments can be cured although some of them may seem to be beyond the scientific knowledge. When people are in short supply of food, they know where to get it from. The churches are busy to mould well – disciplined people who fear God and who can be responsible citizens in thought and deed although some may choose to be deviant.

When God created us, He did not abandon us but it was His plan to be with us always. Our God is the God of history from the beginning to the end of life on earth. Through the institutions in question, people can be trained spiritually intellectually and physically for them to continue to be responsible stewards of God. Through the influence of the inspiration of God the Holy One, those who go through these institutions, are meant to be the light in the darkness of ignorance and unbelief. The objectives of schools and the church are intellectual and spiritual respectively. Let's take advantage of the institutions that help us to read, write and understand the latent treasures in the Holy Bible which are for our salvation. Teachers are the product of schools, colleges and universities according to their passion to equip pupils and students intellectually. All educated people from the nursery schools to the universities came from the tutorship of these noble servants of the people called civil servants. There services deserve very high salaries, unfortunately in some countries, in the world, they are very lowly paid, though properly qualified. These people lead learners from ignorance to the world of enlightenment as the Latin word "Educo" meaning, "I lead from" implies. The word, "Education, is derived from this rich Latin word. All people of different professions came through the tutelage of these humble, diligent, reliable and committed people who hold a good name that calls for their very valuable service to the citizens – the "Civil Servants." Teachers deserve to be respected for the great work they do in the world for the good of humanity.

Although some schools concentrate on subjects centred on mind and body, a human being is body, mind and soul. The soul concentrates on spirituality and morality in light of God the Creator. While the cognitive and applied aspects of education deal with the mind and the body mainly, the cognitive and affective aspects of education lead to applied aspects in training the soul. Facts acquired in biblical studies or theology should influence the soul for the person to put faith into action. Those who need to stay connected to the Creator should have faith in God. Without faith in God, the relationship with the Creator is cut and secular sources become the emphasis in morality. Consequently, unbelief takes roots in the person. Establishing good relationship with God is the way to run away from the deadly sin and God's anger from the Christian point of view.

The writer's experiences as a teacher and ordained Minister, has been noted to be true and to be observed in schools as important educational institutions that team spirit among the teaching staff, respect, honesty, diligence; love of work, students and fellow teachers; self–discipline, meticulous class work planning and marking of the students work collectively, can yield very good results at any school. If a teacher can quickly identify the weaknesses and strengths of the students and help them constantly in their weaknesses, better performance by pupils will be noticed. Observing all these practices, requires love, conscientiousness, patience, endurance and sacrifice. The greatest interest or object of search in education, is to see that students perform well in their studies and succeed in their examinations for a bright future. This is to be valued more than a good salary entitled to be earned by the teacher. The accomplishment of the set "telos" (Greek) – end or goal, brings about bliss to the doer and active participant observers, supervisors, students, general school workers, parents, guardians and the generality of the public.

In some schools, the principals or head teachers and the school development associations devise ways of motivating good teachers to remain in their schools for the good of the students for the preservation of the good name of the school. For extrinsic motivation, teachers can be offered free accommodation and some bonuses. This is a tactful way of maintaining good standards of education at the school. This is the least that the schools can do to motivate the teachers who are valued highly.

Greater motivation lies with the government that has enough financial resources to cater for teachers among its other social responsibilities. The schools as educational institutions should be considered by the government in its budgeting for the education, so that it equips the schools with sufficient school facilities like class text books, library books, computers and sports equipment especially in the third world countries where some financial resources are very scarce. The government should bear in mind that good salaries can incentivise the teaching staff to work harder. Teachers should be treated respectfully for them to enjoy teaching. A favourable environment at any school, yields favourable results for the good of the nation. Unity for the common goal is of necessity in any nation.

Teachers have a noble responsibility that they must carry out sincerely. Children are entrusted to them by the parents to prepare them as the future leaders. Children are the assets of the nation in the entire world and parents invest in their children for a better future, worldwide development and prosperity in different aspects of life. Children therefore, are to be valued and respected highly for what they are and hoped to be in the World. Their contributions will bring joy to all, if they are guided and protected well now. Teachers have to rise above a retrogressive culture of laziness, negligence and apathy for the good of humanity.

Great joy to the teachers comes when they see what their former students are doing in the world. Achievements have long positive effects to the doer in life. This is the joyous experience of the writer who has been a teacher and headmaster in the primary schools from 1963 – 1973; in the high school from 1978 – 1988; at the United theological college, at Hatfield in Harare, Zimbabwe serving as the lecturer and principal of the college from 1990 – 1996. It is something the writer thanks God for in life. To see some of the ex-students and know about their contributions in the world is an admirable contribution to the mother earth. The ex-students are like wealth in the bank of the ex-teacher now, an admirer who sees the contributions the ex-students are making in the world. He finds it a nice and interesting story to tell people repeatedly in his retirement.

As the writer is both a retired teacher and a minister of religion of the United Methodist Church, he sees the complementarity of the school and the church. Both have the teaching and transformational roles for the better spiritually as the church, physically and intellectually as the school. In this unity of the school and the church the holistic teaching of the whole person is fulfilled.

The church and the schools should be seen to be a perfect unit in that those who make up the church were once students. The priests, pastors, ministers, Bishops, Popes and church members first went to a school. When they felt called by God into his Kingdom on earth as followers of Jesus through His prevenient grace call, they were justified because of their penitence or repentance, baptised and became their adopted children of God (John 1:12– 13). Later, those who are converted to Christianity, were confirmed into full membership of the church because of their signs of maturity in their faith and deeds. Doing the will of God is faith or obedience befitting the converted members of the church. These converts worship God individually or corporately to be connected to God their Maker in their attitudes and deeds. They should be humble before God and the people as it is said in the letter of **JAMES 4:10**, *"Humble yourselves before the Lord, and he will lift you up."* God chooses the humble to carry out His mission.

During the writer's school days, the church building was also used as a school building. From sub-A to Standard 3, the writer acquired his education from a church building that had some black boards on the walls. To the people in the community the word church was synonymous to school. When the writer became a trained school teacher, he taught in the schools of the United Methodist Church that could also be used as church buildings (1963 – 73). The church went further to establish mission centres where boarding schools were established. It also established schools in the rural areas to liberate children spiritually and intellectually by teaching scripture or Bible Knowledge and secular subjects. In school time table, Scripture or Bible Knowledge was the first subject to be taught in the morning followed by arithmetic which was thought to require more mental concentration or reasoning than the other subjects that followed. Up to this time, the church in the schools established by the church, work hand in glove in moulding responsible students. The churches that have schools in Zimbabwe have managed to produce many responsible people serving in the world like; Medical doctors, doctors of education, engineers, ministers of religion, accountants, lawyers, business persons, teachers, health workers, architects, social workers, psychologists, farmers and politicians. To rise above culture is to perform better than what is ordinarily expected in life for development and prosperity to be realised.

In Europe very few young people attend church services. Some of the sanctuaries are either almost empty or empty and on market. Youngsters tend to be less religious than their parents. In some cases, where two non-religious parents get married, they transmit their lack of religion in the family. Numerous surveys indicate that some individuals who do not hold religious beliefs are steadily increasing and maybe now representing the majority of the United Kingdom's population. People who say that they do not belong to any religion has risen from 31.4% to 56.6% Between 1983 and 2013 according to the British attitude survey's 31st report issued in 2014. Currently, only 41.7% of people identify themselves as Christians compared to 49.9% in 2008 and 65.2% in 1983. About two centuries ago, Europe was the only continent that was famous for the propagation of the

Christian faith to other continents. Missionaries were involved in mission outreach, to reach out to the countries which had not been converted.

The causes of the decline of Christian faith in Europe I mentioned is said to be atheism, religious tolerance whereby those practices that used to be forbidden earlier on were adopted in the church and secular humanism is in schools. Today, Europe needs massive evangelism to recover the faith of its fathers and fill the sanctuaries. What is happening in Europe is also happening in America where some missionaries went to Africa to evangelise people there.

To rise above culture, there is need to weigh and compare the consequences of the declining of the Christian faith. Is it more advantageous to abandon the Christian faith or not? For Christians, it is better to be obedient to God than not because we were all created for Him. God wants justice and righteousness to prevail on earth (**PSALM 89:14–16**; **AMOS 5:24**). Is the Christian faith not good for spirituality and morality? If it is, then Christianity needs to be adopted for the common good.

Some people feel that Christian believers choose to dissociate themselves from new teachings infiltrating the church. These teachings are incompatible with the teachings of the Bible. They do not want to be forced to tolerate any religious views that are contrary to the fundamental Christian beliefs. Then some teachings that seem to be against the church tradition need to be revisited. Temptations came to Jesus when He was in the wilderness and He emerged victorious as He cited what was written in the scriptures to defeat the devil. Christian believers like other people created in the image of God, are fallible. The spirit of discernment needs to guide the church. God's revelation has been canonised in the Holy Bible (**ROMANS 1:18–32**). The writer is inclined to the United Methodist Church theological principles for doing theology which are:scripture, tradition, experience and reason while other churches have theirs. The attractive theological mantra of Martin Luther, "Sola Scriptura"– The Scriptures only, upholds the authority of the Holy Bible as the only canon for the Christian spirituality and morality. The Holy Bible contains the salvific history of humanity. All things required for the salvation of human beings have been revealed through Jesus Christ, the specific revelation of God, the Father.

The Christian faith in the United States of America is on decline also. The public religion research institutes 2020 centres of America showed that the overall decline of white Christians in America is at 44%, it is said, "3 in 10 US adults are now religious." (14 December 2021). There is a conflict between mainstream American culture and religious beliefs, conflict between religious values and the prevailing culture. When people really just believe, their spiritual enthusiasm to worship their God is automatically quenched. The light of faith in Christians is supposed to be kept burning in hope for a brighter future here on earth and hereafter. Missionaries from Europe and America went to evangelise the Africans and taught them about the Triune God and Salvation from sin and eternal death. What a spiritual wealth was invested in Africa!

Today Africa is said to be predominantly a continent of Christians and Muslims. It is said, according to the updated 2021 data, they are now nearly 685 million Christians in Africa, with 760 million expected by 2025. At least 4 out of 5 Christians in Nigeria, Liberia, Senegal, Cameroon and Chad pray every day. 60% of the Christians in every African country attend church at least weekly. The recent Christian faith growth in Africa is a result of African evangelism and high birth rates. What is good for people is to be preserved because it is valuable but what is bad and against the will of God is to be discarded.

The old established churches:Evangelical Lutheran, Roman Catholic, Anglican, Methodist, Presbyterian, African reformed churches strictly adhere to their traditions. Church doctrines are not to be tempered with to avert heresies that might force the church members out of the church. New religious doctrines should be thoroughly discussed and if they meet the consensus of the majority and in agreement with the will of God, according to the Holy Bible, they can be accepted. Reason rather than emotions should be used in making constructive decisions. Bad decisions and forced beliefs, will destabilise the church and destroy its mission in the world. Since the church is an institution for liberation of people from different types of bondages, they should not tolerate ideas and practices that will entangle it and make it less effective or ineffective to carry out its mission.

To rise above culture, the church should work very hard to break the chains that bind it. The church with control and discerning spirit can destroy the chains. Liberated members of the church should strive to look for the lost and the weak members of the church. It is the truth of God that liberates those who are in spiritual bondages. Jesus once said to some religious leaders "You will know the truth, and the truth will set you free." (John 8:32). To his disciples, the Lord Jesus Christ made himself known in a way that was obscure to them. He said, *"I am the way, the truth and the life. No one comes to the Father except through me"* (John 14:6). God the Father, God the son and God the Holy Spirit are the three persons in one God whom we know as the triune God in our Christian doctrine of Trinity. The three persons are co-eternal. Jesus who referred to Himself as the truth was originally the Word who became flesh in the person of Jesus. This is explained in the doctrine of the incarnation. What was concealed in the Old Testament was revealed in Jesus in the New Testament. The Torah in the Old Testament was superseded by the Son of God who revealed God the Father fully to mankind as He said to Philip, *"Don't you know me, Philip, even after I have been among you such a long time? Anyone who has seen me has seen the Father how can you say, show us the Father? Don't you believe that I am in the Father, and that the Father is in me?"* (**John 14:9-10**).

Christo-centric reflection on religious and social problems can bring about good solutions to utilise. The Omniscient God has answers to our questions on life situations. Since our knowledge is limited, human errors are clear to see or notice in what we do. The gracious Father keeps on guiding and correcting us as He leads us to eternity. Jesus wants us to live in him and he in us to be successful in what we do (**John 15:5**). It is with the assistance of the Holy Spirit that we can understand the word of God and apply it into action to produce good results. The Canon to use in dealing with religious and social matters is the Holy Bible for Christians. As we are living in God's period of grace, we have to make use of it, to correct the past and present mistakes on earth.

The churches was seen to be on the move to reach people in the world in obedience to Jesus' great commission (**Matthew 28:19–20**). When the Lord says "go!" We should go because many people, need to know God's plan for mankind which remains obscure to many. They need to know how they were created and what responsibilities they have to carry out towards God and fellow people. Paul, a great missionary to the gentiles, urged the followers of Jesus to go into the world to teach the word of God for their salvation. He said, *"Consequently, faith comes from hearing the message, and the message is heard through the words about Christ"* (**Romans 10:17**). In **Romans 10:13–15** Paul says, *"For, everyone who calls on the name of the Lord will be saved." How, then, can they call on the one they have not believed in? And how can they believe in the one of whom they have not heard? And how can they hear without someone preaching to them? And how can anyone preach unless they are sent? As it is written: "How beautiful are the feet of those who bring good news!"* Jesus told his followers "The parable of the lost sheep" (**Matthew 18:10–14**) to teach them the need to go and look for the lost, rather than concentrating on the safe sheep that are already in the field at the expense of the Lost. Membership in the church will continue to decline if the church adopts the attitude of "See no evil, hear no evil". This attitude promotes the status quo in the society with people in and outside the church who do what they please. Such an attitude in and outside the church is unbecoming in the sight of God. Disobedience raises the anger of God and is punishable. Those who want to rise above culture, fight to level the ground so that they rise together with others and live comfortably together.

Social and economic stratification

The word stratification means the arrangement or classification of something into groups. A stratum (plural:strata) is a layer of sedimentary rock or soil or igneous rock that was formed at the Earth's surface, with internally consistent characteristics that distinguish it from other layers. A stratum can be seen in almost every country in the world.

Stratum: the level of social class to reach people last signed according to their social status, education or income.

SOCIOLOGICAL CLASSIFICATION OF PEOPLE

	HIGHEST STRATUM	↓ ↑	POWER, RICHEST, PROMOTIONS	← STRATUM
STRATA	MIDDLE STRATUM	↓ ↑	SELF SUFFICIENCE	
	MIDDLE STRATUM	↓ ↑	SELF SUFFICIENCE	
	LOWEST STRATUM	↓ ↑	POVERTY DEPENDENCE	

In each stratum a subculture can be established by a group of people who are accustomed to certain social activities and have the same world views sometimes. To rise from one's stratum to get into a higher Stratum, one must distinguish oneself in having a certain income, power and leadership, education, or promotion. If none of these applies, one remains in the same stratum like the soil stratification in Geography. Utilisation of new ideas can motivate a person to work harder to improve themselves by acquiring education making use of inherent talents to do things for self–improvement. The talented, efficient, diligent, and honest people might be promoted in their workplaces to get into the higher stratum. On the other hand, the lazy ones, the less venturous, the poor filled with the dependancy syndrome end up adopting a subculture that is always retrogressive. They easily accept the status quo. Such people need someone to motivate them for they lack intrinsic motivation. Here, the writer is referring to the able–bodied persons. Those living with disabilities, the aged and the sick within the low stratum are to be cared for by those in higher strata for they have the right to live.

Those in the highest stratum can only remain there if what took them where they are is still functional or effective. If what took them where they are is defunct, the natural way to go is downwards to the middle or lowest stratum. Innovation, diligence, insurance and hope for values to be upheld for those who prefer to rise above culture. History repeats itself but not in the exact way.

Ancient history has a lot for us to learn from. Life was very difficult living in caves, living by hunting using stones for tools and wearing animal skins. People went through the stone and the Iron Ages. They experienced the agrarian revolution when they moved from nomadic life to settlement life and industrial revolution when they had acquired better skills in the invention of machines to use in the manufacturing of equipment and clothes out of wool and cotton. The knowledge that was acquired in the past led further to technological age in which we are.

Rising above culture is to try hard to rise from one stratum higher for better life. However, there are some social evils that can retard some people to rise above culture like oppression of a person by a person. This happens in the employer and employee relationship where the employee trades labour for a wage or salary. Meagre wages paid for long times of hard labour, retard employees to rise from one social stratum to a higher one. Heavy responsibilities that demand heavy economic responses make individuals to rise above culture socially or economically. Poor planning like having many wives and children one cannot look after very well is to be viewed as self–imposed oppression economically. In the past, in other cultures, this practice was emulated because many people in the family, made the work lighter. Since people used to depend on the soil mostly, in a polygamous marriage, a wife would work in a field with her children. At times the harvest would be greater than those realised in the field of the other wives with just a few children. With the inception of urbanisation and migratory labour, bigamous and polygamous families are no longer to be proud of in most cultural circles. It is burdensome to fend for big families. The parents find themselves overstretched economically and at times they end up living beyond their means and in debts. The children do not get enough of what they should have.

There are certain practices that should be abandoned to rise from one social stratum to another to experience development and prosperity in life. We should always move with time that flies. When the writer was a high school student there was a time, he used to joke with fellow students while encouraging one another to study hard. We used to say in Latin "Neglegere opus stultus est." meaning "to neglect work is foolish." When one was given work to do, to neglect it would never give hope to succeed in life but poverty would be a frequent uninvited visitor. As soon as retrogressive tendencies show their heads, they should quickly be nipped in the bud, to rise above a culture of poverty. There are individuals who are interested in socialisation at the expense of working hard for a living in various ways. Our life span is short and yet there is a lot to be done for us to enjoy life given to us by God through his grace that suffices to us all. Self–control is required of us.

Young adults need to work hard in school and outside so that they use their time profitably. Time wasting in peer groups should be avoided. Some behave the way they do because of their good home background economically. They waste their pocket money quickly because they know how to fill their pockets with money again got from unsuspecting parents. Money is not to be wasted but spent carefully to meet the needs. Children who behave as if they are already millionaires drag their parents behind in their social and economic development. In the end they too will be backward in many aspects of life. If your parents are rich, it is not you who is rich. You should aim at working hard in school to have your own things to live on in the future.

Young adults should be good listeners and learners from the experienced adults. Adults have been where they have not been yet. They have experienced what they have not experienced yet. It is said, "experience is the best teacher." The adults have the experience, therefore, have that which makes them good teachers of the inexperienced children. In social groups, people talk about some of the children getting out of hand and others have become social misfits. How can one rise from one social stratum to a higher one with a deviant character? Anyone who loves themselves, they care for their body, soul and mind. That is, they are good stewards of themselves. When young adults get involved in drugs and smoking, they harm themselves and this discredits them from being good stewards of God. Their stagnation in the low stratum will have a long effect in their children if they happen to have to run away from practices that will unnecessarily destroy one's life and engage oneself in legal and gainful activities can raise one to a higher level. To a wild child advice is valued but to a foolish one advice given is like an insult or waste of time, effort or breath. The Holy Bible says what you saw is what you reap. In the letter to the GALATIANS 6:7–8, Paul said, *"Do not be deceived, God cannot be mocked. A man reaps what he sows. The one who sows to please his sinful nature will reap destruction, the one who sought to please the spirit from the spirit will reap eternal life"*

The change of attitude brings about a change of behaviour in a human being. Adoption of high moral standards brings about integrity and respect in any society. Practising doing good things to oneself and others begets a good character and a good character results in trust and acceptability among the people. Actions speak louder than words. People can judge a person by what he says and does. What a person is in his mind can be revealed by what they say or do. When they're quiet and do not do anything, it is difficult to know what kind of people they are. Evil plans first destroy the holders of those plans in that they become the habitual perpetrators of immoral activities which will affect them and others adversely. Those who aim at rising above the bad customs in a culture, will never tire to advise and counsel the doors of bad practices. It is true social interactions that people learn good things that can make them humane in the society. Good conscience changes social deviants as time goes on. If they do not change, they have become addicted to the practices. Individual counselling is good for privacy and group counselling is also good in the form of a general lecture in a seminar. Children are to be jealously guarded against social evils because they are vulnerable.

Children should be taught about the significance of saving money for the future. They can be helped to open their bank accounts in which they can keep their money. This money should be carefully monitored so that withdrawals are not unnecessarily made to avoid bankruptcy and debts in life. Grateful children will start being economically strong when they are still young.

Subsistence farming as in formal education is necessary for children for their social consumption. Such small training will lead to commercial farming when they become adults for self-sufficiency. All these activities are part of proper nurturing of children for good life in future. This is how some of us adults grew up to be responsible people today. In **Proverbs 6:9** an advice to a late bed riser to adopt the attitude of *"Early to bed and early to rise,"* in order to start working early. The writer of the book of Proverbs says in **Proverbs 6:9–10**, *"How long will you lie there, you sluggard? When will you get up from your sleep? A little sleep, a little folding of their hands to rest and poverty will come on you like a thief and scarcity like an armed man."* Diligence is promoted here and those who listen attentively will gain wisdom from such a biblical teaching to avoid creating a retrogressive subculture. To rise above culture is to be alert so that one is not misled by seemingly attractive practices that promote laziness or an idle mind.

There is also need for rest and recreation for children and adults in life. Recreation refreshes the mind and strengthens the body. When parts of the body exercise properly they help in the body functions for good health. Rest is also necessary to regain strength. Physical exercises and games are good practices to relax and keep the body healthy. Physical exercises promote strong muscles and bones. Staying active can also help want to maintain a healthy weight, reduced one's risk for type 2 diabetes, heart disease and reduce the risk for some cancers. Prevention is better than cure to rise above culture is to adopt good practices and leave out bad practices although some people rush for them. Some individuals like those bad practices because they find joy in them and others have been enslaved by them through unnecessary addiction. Let's seek to be liberated rather than to be enslaved by bad habits the robbers of our freedom in life.

We should not forget to eat balanced diet for good health. Some foods are not good for our bodies; therefore, we should not be tempted to take them. There are some foods we can live without taking them, with no adverse results whereas others cause some physical deficiencies if not eaten. A balanced diet supplies the nutrients the body needs to work effectively. Without balanced nutrition the bodies open to diseases, infection, fatigue and low performance. Children who like healthy food might face growth and developmental problems, poor academic performance and frequent infections. Taking the right amount of calories for the work one does will balance the energy one consumes with the energy one uses. Eating or drinking more than one's body needs, one will put on weight because the energy one does not use is stored as fat.

Drunkenness and gluttony are forbidden in the Bible (**Proverbs 23:20–21**), *"Do not join those who drink too much wine or gorge themselves on meet for drunkards and gluttons become poor, and drowsiness clothes them in rags."* Eating in moderation is required for healthy eating. Scriptures and science agree in the expression of the truth. To rise above culture is to be obedient to biblical and health instructions.

To be included in healthy living is cleanliness. It is said by people, "cleanliness is next to godliness." By this it is meant that people have a moral duty to keep themselves in their homes clean. To avoid diseases and infections it is important to have a clean environment. Clothes, utensils, food, shelter and the body should be kept clean. Fresh air should be allowed in the dwelling place. All these things are to be done for the welfare of the people and to maintain a high standard of healthy living.

All in all, the account on "rising above culture," aims at urging people to do their best in all aspects of life and leave the impossibilities to God. The God we worship is the God of the things that cannot be solved by the natural power of human beings which is given to them by God himself. This is why we talk about miracles in the Bible and even in today's life. When God intervenes in difficult times, we realise his intervention in the termination of those situations. When God orders the life-threatening situations to halt, even nature obeys (**Matthew 8:23–27**, **Mark 4:35–41**, **Luke 8:23–25**, **John 11:40–44**). Today even some doctors are surprised by some healings they make in the hospitals that seemed to be beyond their medical recorded accounts. Such events can be interpreted as miracles. With God's help, human beings can do things that are beyond our understanding for our mutual good. The source of knowledge and wisdom that we have is God who gives them graciously to us. Through these God-given gifts, discoveries, inventions, impressive performances in sports and games are noted in life.

In some of their elementary schools, pupils are encouraged to work hard in class by reciting a motivating poem which goes like this:

> "Good better best
> Never let it rest
> Till the good is better
> And the better best"

It is good to do good but there is room to do better and the best in life. Culture is dynamic. Cultures need to assimilate good customs and get rid of the bad ones to improve socially, religiously, politically and economically. Failure to correct sinful practices to please God, is sinning through omission or passing judgement on ourselves as expressed in the gospel according to **John 3:19–21**, *"This is the verdict:Light has come into the world, but people love darkness instead of light because their deeds were evil. Everyone who does evil hates the light, and will not come into the light for fear that their deeds will be exposed. But whoever lives by the truth comes into the light, so that it may be seen plainly that what they have done has been done in the sight of God."* the choice we make and put into practice predetermines the verdict in any court of law and before the righteous and just God now and at the end of time.

People should put their talents into practice to avoid negligence of their responsibilities and blame that follows their negligence. Failure to use one's talent, will result in negative consequences as what Jesus taught in his parable of the talents found in the gospel according to **Luke 19:11–27** and **Matthew 25:14–30**. All people have some talents which are latent to those who have not discovered their talents yet. These talents should be utilised to yield the required results. We depend on God–given talents for our existence on earth. Correctness is reached by reasoning but follows logical thinking to its end. Lack of reasoning leaves things half done or inconclusive and as a result, the intended purpose of reasoning is not reached as is the case in mathematics and sciences.

In rising above culture, maximisation of the talents or knowledge leads to discoveries, inventions and transformation of the world views of the people. Like in geography, people first believed that the world was flat and at the end of the earth were some waterfalls. This kind of thinking was mythical, and it retarded the discoveries of other lands beyond people's horizons. Courage and the passion to discover the unknown through navigation proved the people's concept of the earth wrong for, after all, the world is round. Navigating eastward led the sailor to where they started by sailing through the West. It is believed that Pythagoras first proposed that the earth was round around 500 B.C. Around 350 B.C Aristotle declared that the new earth was a sphere. The most noted Portuguese sailor Fernai de Magalhaes "Magellan" Circumnavigated the world from 1519 to 1522 proving the world is round. Without rising above culture, the wonders of the earth remain unknown.

Check your record

Do you know who you are inwardly and outwardly? Do you know your spiritual, moral, physical, mental strengths and weaknesses you should work on as a good steward of God in the world? Do you know that what you are is not what you ought to be?

Ideas emanating from our environment and spiritual world that invade us can change our attitudes and behaviour adversely. People who were formally good in attitude and behaviour can be turned to be bad as they tend to be cruel or unmerciful, hateful, harmful, deceitful, cunning, lying, corrupt, conceited murderers, idolators, thieves and many other immoral things.

God would like us to take after Him so that we can maintain a good relationship with Him spiritually and morally. God is holy. He does not compromise with sin that corrupts, hence people created in the image of God should run away from sin that severs good relationship and leads into eternal death. Through faith in the Triune God people can enjoy the good relationship and peace with Him which leads to eternal life. When we sin in word, thought and deed, we should remorsefully repent and ask for the forgiveness of our sins wholeheartedly from God to have our good relationship with Him re-established. Jesus Christ, the greatest teacher who has ever lived on earth, taught His followers in His sermon on the mount about their spiritual and moral status as children of God to be like God: *"Be perfect therefore, as your heavenly Father is perfect"* (**MATTHEW 5:48**). True peace with God and among people can prevail if we behave like God to God Himself and fellow people on earth. When we turn away from God, we will conform to the world and seek to please ourselves and oppress or abuse fellow people in various ways. To do so is to fight against God. When we profess to know God and we are truly His children, we should refrain from ill-treating fellow people and promote the ethical principle of LOVE which is AGAPE in Greek language. This is the love that God loves us with. It is unconditional love; the love that loves despite anything (**MATTHEW 5:43–48**).

We are quick to see how fellow people wrong us as we are enveloped in false self-righteousness. The perfect mirror for our own righteousness is Jesus, the perfect revelation of God to mankind who is co-eternal with God the Father and formally known as "The Word" (**JOHN 1:1–5**). Self-introspection which is unbiased can expose our shortfalls clearly from which we should repent to be strong spiritually and morally to the joy of God our Maker for whom we were Created. To do His will is to please Him. Going to church while our hearts are impervious to God's truth, is a futile spiritual exercise that makes us move in circles without reaching the intended destination.

Observing the spiritual and moral principle of LOVE, helps us to rise above any culture. We become the salt of the world by preserving our Christian virtues which are spiritual and ethical values seen in light of Jesus for the good of humanity. We also become the light of the world as we guide fellow people to adopt good attitudes and behaviour towards God and fellow people, as citizens of God's Kingdom on earth. The devil is always busy tempting us to abandon the divine responsibilities given to us by God for us to be like him in attitude and behaviour towards God, our Maker and fellow people. To be faithful or truthful to God and the people, we should seek to cling to the word of God which is the liberating truth from sin (**JOHN 8:14–59**).

Christians should observe the two types of relationships which are the vertical between God and the self and the horizontal which is between the self and other people. One who says they love God and worship Him but hate others on ethnic, tribal, religious, and political grounds are not in good standing with God. Anything good we do to fellow people; we do to God and anything bad we do to them we do to God also. When we worship God, give Him His honour by obeying Him that is good for that is what God expects of us. When we observe justice as we live amongst ourselves, that is good that is what is expected of us to do amongst ourselves. In **Amos 5:24** we read thus: *"But let justice roll on like a river, righteousness like a never–failing stream!"* Justice deals with how we live in good relationship among ourselves. What is good is good and what is bad is bad no matter who does it. Where there is justice, all are under the law which corrects them, human life is valued and peace is upheld. In righteousness, right relationship with God should be maintained by honouring or obeying Him as our Lord and the Sovereign Ruler of the universe. Righteousness and justice should prevail among people who seek to please God and the people in the world. When we follow the word of God, there will be peace, social development and prosperity in the world.

In dealing with other people while having ulterior selfish motives, we tend to amass wealth at the expense of others. We deliberately impoverish others by taking away what is genuinely supposed to be theirs for existence because of selfishness. Such attitudes and behaviour are unbecoming in the sight of God. This is why we need to repent here on earth and before we die for there is no repentance after death. Christian ethics encourage us to be good, right, loving and people of integrity for the welfare of mankind. Let's adopt the attitude of running away from sin and anger of God caused by our own sins. We should hunger after righteousness to be fed on the righteous spiritual food by God (**Luke 6:21**).

The decalogue as the will of God

The decalogue for the chosen people of God is given in **Exodus 20:3–17** and is made up of ten commandments. The first four commandments are related to the people's vertical relationship with God whereas the last six commandments are related to the horizontal relationship among human beings. The first four commandments are for people's good relationship with God whereas the remaining six commandments are for justice or sound relationship among people as they co-exist in the world. Following the will of God by observing the commandments can help us to correct ourselves in order to please God.

In Christianity, the decalogue should not only remain on paper to remind us how we should behave but to be internalised to be our custom. To be saved from sin and eternal death after the resurrection of dead, is through faith in Jesus and by God's grace (**JOHN 3:16**). The decalogue is the Old Testament or Covenant but perfection is not within range of human possibility. The Apostle Paul in his letter to the **ROMANS 3:21–26** affirms that our salvation from sin is through faith in Jesus who supersedes the decalogue for He sacrificially died for all people to redeem them from sin. John the Baptist affirmed the messiahship of Jesus when he said, *"Look, the Lamb of God, who takes away the sin of the world!"* (**JOHN 1:29**). On our own, we cannot be perfect through acts of charity but through faith in Jesus, the perfect one, as we strive to live a clean life in thought, word and deed through the life and teachings of Jesus. Christo-centric ethics are essential for those who would like to live above retrogressive cultures. Those who want to follow Jesus should learn to live sacrificial lives which call for selflessness in attitudes and behaviour as is stated in **MATTHEW 16:24**, *"Then Jesus said to his disciples, "Whoever wants to be my disciples must deny themselves and take up their cross and follow me."*

God calls people to be His co-workers to transform the world to be a better place to live in. People living in faith are supposed to have a foretaste of heavenly life where there is faithfulness, joy and peace eternally. Life on earth should be viewed as just temporary and a preparation for eternity. During the short time we have on earth we should work diligently in order to earn our living faithfully for our good and others. God is involved in our social activities to guide and protect us to reach our destinies. God encourages us to do good of any kind to all the people always. He reminds us what He expects us to do to Him and fellow people. When we refuse to do His will, we find ourselves entangled in social calamities or misfortunes that corrupt us in different aspects of life. In life we will meet some temptations that can be overcome through faith in the Triune God. These temptations are caused by the devil who misleads us spiritually and morally. There are times when we are tempted by our own desires to the extent of doing unethical deeds to satisfy our own selfish desires. Temptations lead to spiritual enslavement or sin and death (JOHN 1:13– 15).

Divine warning to mankind

To be forewarned, is to be forearmed to avoid disastrous results. Choosing to do the right things in God's name is ethically and joyfully acceptable by God who blesses us abundantly in response. Negative responses to divine warnings raise the anger of God. It is wise to run away from the anger of God by doing what pleases Him. We must adopt an attitude of doing things with clear and innocent conscience for God the Holy One to rise above retrogressive and destructive cultural practices. Doing things with ulterior evil motives to please ourselves or others deceitfully, can be exposed by the omniscient God to the perpetrators and the victims through their conscience to their agonising shame or regret. Those who listen to the whispering word of God, repent but the impenitent ones continue to do what pleases them though against the will of God to face the fatal anger of God.

Let's take God's warnings to us for they are said in His holiness and justice for our good. The Holy Bible abounds with these warnings for our own spiritual and ethical maturity and salvation from sin. Some of them are:Noah's warning of the flood, warnings about the evil practices of the Canaanites as stated in DEUTERONOMY 18:9: *"When you enter the land the Lord your God is giving you, do not learn to imitate the detestable ways of the nations there,"* the book of Proverbs which is the book of wisdom states clearly the detestable things to God which should be avoided. These are things that should be avoided by those who emulate to rise above destructive and backward social practices in the society. They are laid down in PROVERBS 6:16–19. God knows all our plans and is against the evil ones.

Those who want to rise above destructive customs should be aware of these bad practices to please God and to cultivate morally acceptable practices in the community where they live. In the society you happen to live in be quick to find out people who are more inclined to bad practices and refrain to follow suit. In **DEUTERONOMY 20:18**, we read thus, *"Otherwise, they will teach you to follow all detestable things they do in worshipping their gods and you will sin against the Lord your God."*

In His salvific history, God sent prophets to warn the chosen people against abandoning the covenant He made with them to maintain the right relationship with Him. Through the New Testament, Jesus Christ the perfect revelation of God to mankind, taught about God, His Kingdom, what God Himself expects the citizens of His Kingdom to do for their salvation from sin and eternal death. Jesus' disciples and apostles affirmed the teachings of Jesus to their followers to strengthen their faith in God through Jesus, His only begotten Son and through whom all things were made (**JOHN 1:1–4**). Paul, writing to Timothy in **2 TIMOTHY 3:16–17** said, *"All scripture is God– breathed and is useful for teaching rebuking, correcting and training in righteousness, so that the servant of God may be thoroughly equipped for every good work."*

Self–introspection is necessary for any leader of integrity in the society to lead by example spiritually and morally. Although we are not perfect on our own, we need to strive to live a clean life. The fruits of the Holy Spirit should be manifested in our life as alluded to in Paul's letter to the **GALATIANS 5:22–23**, *"But the fruit of the Spirit is love, joy, peace, forbearance, kindness, goodness, faithfulness, gentleness and self–control. Against such things there is no law."*

In His sermon on the mount, Jesus gave an ethical teaching on self–introspection in **MATTHEW 7:5** where He said, *"You hypocrite, first take the plank out of your own eye, and then you will see clearly to remove the speck from your brother's eye."* What Jesus says and does is the right thing to follow for He says and does it in agreement with His Father in heaven as is expressed in **JOHN 14:31**, *"But he comes so that the world may learn that I love the Father and do exactly what my Father has commanded me."* When we are more inclined to vice than to virtue, it is very difficult to practice Christo–centric ethics. However, Jesus ceaselessly calls mankind to learn from Him, to be good followers and doers of social practices or customs befitting the children of God. In **Matthew 11:28–30** Jesus said, *"Come to me, all you who are weary and burdened, and I will give you rest. Take my yoke upon you and learn from me, for I am gentle and humble in heart, and you will find rest for your souls. For my yoke is easy and my burden is light."*

Believing in God seems to be burdensome and restrictive and yet it is lighter than carrying a burden of sins that torment the body, mind and soul, and leads to eternal death. Believing in God yields self-control, courage, perseverance, joy, rest and hope for salvation and eternal life hereafter. God's reward to those who believe in Him, is much greater than any wealth that a person can have on earth. It is much greater than material reward that can be given to a person by another person on earth.

One who aims to rise above culture should be religiously influenced by the sacrificial, spiritual and righteous goal that can be reached through faith in Jesus and by God's grace, as is alluded to in the book of **John 3:16**, *"For God so loved the world that He gave His one and only Son, that whoever believes in him shall not perish but have eternal life."* Paul instructing the Ephesians in living a righteous life in **Ephesians 4:17–19** said, *"So, I tell you this, and insist on it in the Lord, that you must no longer live as the Gentiles do, in the futility of their thinking. They are darkened in their understanding and separated from the life of God because of the ignorance that is in them due to the hardening of their hearts. Having lost all sensitivity so as to indulge in every kind of impurity, and they are full of greed."*

Spiritual rebirth is a necessity

To live a righteous life acceptable to God according to Christianity is to be reborn spiritually as affirmed in the Gospel according to **John 1:12–13**. *"Yet to all who did receive him, he gave the right to become children of God– children born not of natural descent, nor of human decision or a husband's will, but born of God."* In **John 3:3,** Jesus said, *"Very truly I tell you, no one can see the kingdom of God unless they are born again. To be born again is to accept Jesus as your personal Saviour and get baptised in the name of God the Father; God the Son and God the Holy Spirit."*

This religious phenomenological practice of baptism is an indication of the death of the old self and rebirth of the new self spiritually by God's justifying grace. A person accepted by God in this way, becomes a child of God by adoption and co-heir with Jesus Christ (**Romans 8:17**). Living a righteous or clean life, is a practice required of a person who is born again to please God and to be a strong and faithful messenger of God in the transformation of human minds and ways of relating to God and fellow people in the world. Theologically, a born-again person, has a deep knowledge of the fact that all people were created in God's image for God Himself. People are supposed to do the will of God in life for their righteousness, justice, peace, joy, social development and prosperity. Jesus taught His disciples to ask in prayer, for the will of God to be done on earth as it is done in heaven (**Matthew 6:10**). When our will is against the will of God, ours should give way to that of God for our personal good and for the good of others. Such theological reasoning in decision-making establishes good and right theological ethics for our God, the Sovereign Ruler.

Paul in **Romans 6:1-24**, teaches the born-again people how they should behave in their new status to identify themselves with the death and resurrection of Jesus. The born-again Christians should be dead to sin and alive in Christ in attitudes and behaviour. Paul warns the Christians in Rome in **Romans 12:2** against conforming to this world which has so many things that are so tempting to the extent of destroying our faith in God. Self-control and a discerning spirit are to be put into practice for our safety and well-being. Questions in decision-making are to be asked and sincerely answered such as, what is right or wrong; Good or bad; just or unjust; fitting or unfitting? After asking each of these questions there is yet another question to be answered to vindicate our chosen decision to take and the question is, why? This last question seeks to find out the authority behind my decision like, Theology, Science, conscience, tradition, law, proved educational principles and situation. Paul said, *"Do not conform to the pattern of this world, but be transformed by the renewing of your mind. Then you will be able to test and approve what God's will is– his good, pleasing and perfect will."*

Theocentric (centred on God) practices lead to Christian eschatological beliefs (beliefs about death, judgement and final destiny of individual souls and humankind). "Where will you spend eternity?" This is the question to be answered in light of God and what we do on earth. At the end of the known time, there will be the Judgement Day when God in His Son Jesus Christ, will execute His justice to the nations of the world. The justice of God is two sided– justification and condemnation according to what people did on earth (**Matthew 25:31–46**; **Revelation 22:12–16**).

Be a good shepherd

To rise above culture like Jesus, believers in Jesus should adopt Christlike characteristics to genuinely please God and the people with clear conscience. What the Christians should bear in mind is that the mission of Jesus is the mission of the church (**Luke 4:18–19**; **Matthew 28:18– 20**). The theology of liberation from all types of human bondages physically, mentally, and spiritually should be aimed at. In **John 10:11–18**, Jesus taught people about Himself as the good shepherd. This teaching is the model of a good shepherd for the Christians. Jesus said in **John 10:11**, *"I am the good shepherd. The good shepherd lays down his life for the sheep."* Sacrificial life is required of the followers of Jesus who serve the people in humility to the extent of even dying for them. Many Christians have died in the hands of antagonists, as martyrs because of their adherence to their Christian beliefs. Selflessness for the good of others, is one of the sacrificial characteristics of good shepherds in the society. The shepherding principle of practical theology, is risky in that protecting the people who are metaphorically called the sheep, is like fighting against the predators that are eager to destroy them. Telling people, the truth that can liberate them from vices can easily be misconstrued as inciting them to rise against the authorities under whose jurisdiction they live. On the other hand, to be silent when people are prejudiced is to support the status–quo and is against the will of God. Compromising with sinful activities is sinning through omission. Good leaders or believers seek to please God rather than conceding to the corrupt wills, and deeds of the people. This is done by believers in Jesus Christ in their endeavour to live a clean life. Peace is a Christian virtue which should be upheld in the world for it is conducive to social development and prosperity. Jesus said in His sermon on the mount, *"Blessed are the peacemakers, for they will be called children of God. Blessed are those who are persecuted because of righteousness for theirs is the kingdom of heaven"* (Matthew **5:10–11**).

Living in obedience to God

We need God in our lives to transform from what we are to what we ought to be in attitudes and behaviour or character. When God intervenes in our life situations, changes for the better can be experienced to our surprise, peace and joy as we coexist on earth.

The writer feels uplifted spiritually by the hymn: "***I Need Thee Every Hour.***" This hymn exposes deep transforming feelings of a believer sung thus:

[1] I need Thee every hour
Most gracious Lord
No tender voice like Thine
Can peace afford

[2] I need Thee every hour
Stay Thou nearby
Temptations lose their power
When Thou art nigh

Refrain

I need Thee, oh, I need Thee
Every hour I need Thee
Oh, bless me now Saviour
I come to Thee

[3] I need Thee every hour
In joy or pain
Come quickly and abide
Or life is vain

Refrain

⁴ I need Thee, oh, I need Thee
Every hour, I need Thee
Oh, bless me now, my Saviour
I come to Thee

God is the people's unfailing inspirer and enabler in making good decisions and doing good things for their benefit. The Triune God is the source of all wisdom for the spiritual and moral welfare of mankind because He is eternally holy and omniscient. By His grace, He endows people with various mental capabilities which can be used to shape up the world to be a better place to live in, if they choose to be people of integrity. We are what we are by nature and choice. Good or bad ideas and practices we adopt tend to characterise us. As we live, there is always room for us to be better people, as we move towards what we ought to be. Let us aspire to rise above retrogressive culture that is infected with unbecoming social practices that God abhors.

Take a stand in Jesus and you will not go wrong

Take a stand in Jesus the perfect revelation of God the Father to mankind and you will not go wrong. Since the Triune God is holy, He cannot be the source of anything evil. When decisions are infiltrated by the selfish or corrupt human ideas, they become misleading, dangerous or fatal. All sinful acts come out of corrupt personal or social decisions. Many people have suffered or are still suffering because of bad decisions for self-appeasement.

Serious Theocentric or Christocentric ethics emanate from profound faith in the Triune God, the Maker of heaven and earth, for whom mankind were made. To transform the world in different aspects of life, people need to work in consultation with God. In **PROVERBS 11:14**, we are advised to seek advice to come out with good decisions: *"For lack of guidance a nation falls, but victory is won through many advisors."* The advisors whose source of wisdom is God, give constructive pieces of advice to the decision makers for the good of the people. Those who take a stand in Jesus, will stand for the truth although it is opposed by many people. This is when democracy can suffer a defeat. Many people who are in support of evil things can be defeated by a few people who stand for the truth as long as God is on their side. Here, it is God who will fight for the few in defence for the truth. Elisha advised his servant *"Don't be afraid," the prophet answered, "Those who are with us are more than those who are with them." And Elisha prayed, "Open his eyes, Lord, so that he may see." Then the Lord opened the servant's eyes, and he looked and saw the hills full of horses and chariots of fire all around Elisha,"* **2 Kings 6:16–17**.

A few people with God on their side, far outnumber many people who fight against the truth. Paul in his letter to the **Romans 8:33–34** says, *"Who will bring any charge against those whom God has chosen? It is God who justifies. Who then is the one who condemns? No one, Christ Jesus who died– more than that, who was raised to life is at the right hand of God and is also interceding for us."* The influence of the truthful people who advocate for righteousness and justice will continuously impact the wayward people until they come to their senses and accept the truth that liberates from mental and spiritual myopic bondages. However, there may be those who may choose to be impervious to facts and continue to act according to their misdirected conscience to their own peril here on earth or hereafter, at the end of the known time.

Hunger and thirst after righteousness

In His sermon on the mount, Jesus said, *"Blessed are those who hunger and thirst for righteousness, for they will be filled"* (**Matthew 5:6**). Spiritual hunger and thirst are the passion to be in right relationship with God. Such a spiritual condition can only be satisfied through faith in God Himself. Those who open their hearts will receive what they need from God who is the source of everything that is wise and good for our life. John, the disciple of Jesus said, *"This is the message we have heard from him and declare to you: God is light; in Him is no darkness at all. If we claim to have fellowship with him and yet walk in the darkness, we lie and do not live out the truth. But if we walk in the light, as he is in light, we have fellowship with one another, and the blood of Jesus, his Son purifies us from all sin"* (**1 John 1:5–7**).

People tend to nod their heads clap their hands, even ululate in support of a misleading idea or practice, said or done by one they love or idolise consciously or otherwise. Here Christians pretend to see no sin to please the speaker or leader. Have Christians, enveloped in the politicians' propaganda, not made the lives of other people so difficult and miserable because of their misleading utterances and deeds? How can people who walk in the light of God express hatred to fellow citizens on political grounds? Do people see things eye to eye always? We need to repent from sin. The ethical principle of agapeic love makes people to be tolerant and patient to bring about true unity, peace, development and prosperity through reconciliation.

To know God and do what He says is to be liberated spiritually. Those who are liberated walk in the light taking after their heavenly Father. Let's learn from Jesus about true spiritual liberation that people need in JOHN 8:12, *"I am the light of the world. Whoever follows me will never walk in darkness but will have the light of life."* Ignorance and sinfulness make even believers lose sight of the truth that liberates. Jesus who said, *"I am the light of the world,"* becomes spiritually obscure and irrelevant to those who refuse to accept Him. In JOHN 8:31–32, we read: *"To the Jews who had believed him, Jesus said, "If you hold to my teaching, you are really my disciples. Then you will know the truth, and the truth will set you free."* Understanding who Jesus Christ is and what He can do for mankind through faith in Him, can liberate us spiritually from sin. In JOHN 14:6–7, it is said to Thomas, *"I am the way and the truth and the life. No one comes to the Father except through me. If you really know me, you will know my Father as well. From now on, you do know him and have seen him."* The writer, urges mankind to rise above culture by trusting God and aspiring to do His will as has been revealed to us all in Jesus. We should love all people as God loves them but dislike their evil deeds from which they should repent.

Jesus, the greatest teacher because He came from the Father and is co-eternal with God the Father and God the Holy Spirit, spoke about heavenly things in simple earthly stories called parables for people to understand the concealed heavenly and earthly things for them to act wisely and responsibly in making their decisions in this world that has many temptations caused by the devil and ourselves (JAMES 1:13–15; 1 CORINTHIANS 1:11–13). Jesus, the Son of God was tempted by Satan to abandon His mission in the world to engage in earthly activities to the detriment of mankind. Providing food to the people only will not lead them to eternal life, entertaining people to satisfy their curiosity will not lead people to heaven, political power though good to get people organised for earthly life, if done in the spirit of God, does not lead to heaven for people shall not live by bread alone but also by the word of God that sustains the soul in good relationship with God the creator. It is God alone who should be worshipped on earth. The earthly rulers, no matter how powerful or popular they may be, they are mortal beings and fallible. God alone who is immortal and infallible is to be worshipped. Jesus overcame Satan and his temptations and clang to the mission of God His Father (Missio Dei – Latin) to preach, teach people about God's kingdom and to suffer vicariously in His life until His death on the cross as an expiation of people's sins. Through faith in Jesus alone there is life in eternity by God's grace (JOHN 3:16).

Time came for Jesus to warn His followers to beware of temptations that come stealthily to dissuade inattentive people and mislead them to do what they ought not to do. Jesus said, *"Watch and pray so that you will not fall into temptation"* (MATTHEW 26:41). People need to be connected to God in order to be watchful or vigilant and to be ready to defend themselves against Satan or demons. As they remain watchful, they should also be prayerful– watch and pray "vigilate et orate" (Latin).

The followers of Jesus called Christians who form the body of Jesus Christ, should be prayerful to stay connected to God. Any time is prayer time in order to have special time with God to dialogue with Him. We are co-heirs (ROMANS 8:7) with Jesus Christ our prayerful Lord and Saviour who defeated sin and death for our sake (1 CORINTHIANS 15:3–4). The Triune God is incorruptible. On top of His cross where He was nailed was the label written in Latin:

"Iesus Nazareus Rex Iudaeorum– INRI" meaning Jesus of Nazareth King of the Jews. The King of kings and the Lord of lords was nailed knowingly and unknowingly by the persecutors but He proved invincible. God is invincible. This Jesus who died and was buried, resurrected from the dead as He won the victory for mankind. He declared our liberation from sin and death on the cross when He shouted "Tetelestai!" which was Greek for "paid in full." The debt of our sins was paid in full by Jesus on the cross for us to be saved through faith in Jesus Himself and by God's grace.

Gone Is All My Debt of Sin

[1] Gone is all my debt of sin,
A great change is wrought within
And to live I now begin,
Risen from the fall;
Yet the debt I did not pay
Someone died for me one day,
Sweeping all the debt away
Jesus paid it all

Refrain

Jesus died and paid it all, yes,
On the cross of calvary, oh
And my stony heart was melted
At His dying, dying call;
Oh, His heart in shame was broken on the tree for you and me, yes
And the debt, the debt is cancelled
Jesus paid it, paid it all

[2] Oh, I hope to please Him now,
Light of joy is on my brow,
Safe within His love,
Making His, the debt I owed
Freedom true He has bestowed;
So, I'm singing on the road
To my home above.

³ Sinner, not for me alone
Did the Son of God atone;
Your debt, too, He made His own,
On the cruel tree

⁴ Come to Him with all your sin;
Be as white as snow within;
Full salvation you may win
And rejoice with me.

Source: "The Cyber Hymnal #10148
Author:M.S. Shaffer

What Jesus did for the entire world and the apocalyptic concept of life in eternity, had and still has a great persuasion on many people who decided and still decide to be penitent with the author, being no exception. "Gone Is All My Debt of Sin," is explanatory of our redemption by God's grace and it is as inspiring to draw people to God with praises and gratitude. Such an approach in the evangelisation of people, is very effective in encouraging people to rise above culture in spirituality and social ethics. The achievement of the utmost spiritual goal, that is, God's justification by His grace on the Judgement Day brings about everlasting joy to live with God eternally. Apocalyptic teachings in the book of Revelation give hope to believers in Jesus.

Reading the Bible gives hope, courage, patience and endurance in times of difficulties and persecution for God is very close to the sufferers, comforting and encouraging them to cling to their faith. The sufferers are among those Jesus came for into the world to save them besides being liberated spiritually, psychologically and physically (LUKE **4:18–19**), God fights wars for the voiceless in different ways to save His own people or children though they may be persecuted to death. Persecutors can destroy the body but not the soul which can only be destroyed together with the body in hell by the Almighty God alone (LUKE **12:4–7**).

Knowing who you are and whose you are, why you were created, what you should do to please God, what you should do and where you hope to be after life on earth will help you to live a responsible life on earth. Jesus demonstrated the significance of humbleness before God and people as expressed by Paul in his letter to the PHILIPPIANS 2:5, *"In your relationships with one another, have the same mindset as Christ Jesus who, being in very nature God, did not consider equality with God something to be used to his own advantage; rather, he made himself nothing by taking the very nature of a servant, being made in human likeness, and being found in appearance as a man he humbled himself by becoming obedient to death. Therefore, God exalted him to the highest place and gave him the name that is above every name, that is the name of Jesus every knee should bow in heaven and on earth and under the earth, and every tongue acknowledge that Jesus Christ is Lord, to the glory of God the Father."*

Humbleness coupled with faith makes a stable believer in attitude and behaviour towards God and the people. Believers with such virtuous characteristics are aided by self–control which is also a Christian virtue. The committed humble believer gets wisdom from God to be a doer of faith, that is they rise above culture and help to bring people to Christ by using various gifts of the Holy Spirit. Let us discover our talents and make use of them to be faithful servants of God in the world. When we draw closer to God in faith, He draws closer to us and gives us the wisdom we need to serve Him and the people as what is said in JEREMIAH 33:3, *"Call to me and I will answer you, and tell you great and unsearchable things you do not know."* The world we live in needs God more than the earthly things, in order to use these earthly things responsibly to benefit all people irrespective of their social status in life.

God as the Sovereign Ruler

God as the Sovereign Ruler loves us all and He expects us all to reciprocate His love, living as responsible and humane citizens among ourselves. A lesson can be learnt from the contemporary Pharisees of Jesus themselves, they were pietistic in character and wanted to live within the confinement of the law of God. When they encountered Jesus, they wanted to test his knowledge about God and His will for the people under

His rule. Their question of Jesus was about the greatest law to be followed by believers in one true God, the Creator of heaven and earth. Jesus without mincing His words told them convincingly the first law and the second one that was like the first one, two of which showed the vertical and horizontal relationships that should be observed by believers in God to be called good and obedient children and servants of God hoping to inherit God's Kingdom. Jesus briefly said in response, *"Love the Lord your God with all your heart and with all your soul and mind. This is the first and greatest commandment and the second is like it, "Love your neighbour as yourself. All the Law and the Prophets hang on these two commandments"* **MATTHEW 22:37–40**.

By Jesus summary of the decalogue, the Pharisees were convinced beyond any doubt that Jesus had profound knowledge of the law. What the Pharisees did not know about Jesus is the truth that He was the Messiah, and the Son of God they were waiting for to liberate them from the foreign rule. When Jesus asked His questioners about the Messiah and the prophecy of David concerning the Messiah which they failed to answer, they departed from Him and they did not dare to ask Him some questions lest they might only succeed to expose their ignorance further about the concept of Christology (Person, nature and role of Christ).

When people do not know the truth, they go by assumptions or myths to satisfy their curiosity and imaginations as rational beings. When they keep on guessing they make minor and great mistakes which have equal consequences to God, themselves and others with whom they live in the society. Consequently, there is need to search for ways of harmonising people to know the will of God to operate in love and peace in their daily activities in light of God, our Sovereign Ruler and the source of life which we enjoy on earth.

Our Sovereign Ruler who is Yahweh is invisible but His activities are visible and acknowledgeable. We live and work because of His unmerited grace without which we cease to live. He is Jehovah Jireh because He provides all things we need. He is Jehovah Nissi because He fights battles for us in life like ailments, starvation, poverty, ignorance, oppression, and sin. He is Jehovah Rapha for he heals us when we are sick with or without the help of medication for, He speaks things into being.

Nature is under His control. He speaks and nature listens like human beings and takes the Lord's commands. When we are healed in the hospitals God is there because He is omnipresent. The doctors and medicine are His for the latter are extracted from the medicinal plants created by God for our use. Our Sovereign Ruler is caring. When we die even if the doctors and medicine are there, this is the natural way we depart from earth as arranged by our Maker (Ecclesiastes 3:1–2; Psalm 103:15–16; Job 14:1–5).

According to Christian Theology, there is life in heaven beyond earthly life which can be given to those who believe in God through Jesus Christ who resurrected from the dead (John 3:16). God is El Roi (The God who sees me), we cannot hide away from Him. He sees the situations we may be in like being sick, hungry, poor, oppressed, discriminated or murdered. He intervenes in all human life situations to liberate us since He is the gracious God. He can send some empathetic and benevolent people who see the plight of others and provide what is needed. God is El Shaddai (God Almighty). He is invincible (Deus Invictus Est– Latin). All earthly powers put together cannot overpower Him because He is immortal whereas human beings are mortal. God is also known by other names that show His greatness in heaven and on earth. Because of what God is all the people on earth ought to worship Him. Although God is almighty, He is just and loving to allow people to make up their decisions whether to obey or disobey Him. However, negative response of people to His revelation which is unbelief, is punishable at the end of life on earth for our failure to take heed of what God has told us through General Revelation and Specific Revelation (John 14:6–14; Romans 1:18–32; 2:1–16). Because God is love (1 John 4:16), believers and non-believers enjoy God's grace for the air is provided to all the people irrespective of their beliefs or devoid of them, it rains for us all and at times, the non-believers can be wealthier than believers. It is what we decide to do to God and the people on which the final judgement will be based by God. (Matthew 25:31–46; Matthew 6:24). What you do with the wealth you accumulate rightfully in the sight of God, will be determined by God, right or wrong. Money acquired corruptly but shared to people generously will not merit God's favour to the donor because of how it was acquired.

Rulers under the righteous Sovereign Ruler of the universe are allowed to rule on behalf of God, righteously and justly as what He does. He enthrones and dethrones them in different ways as He pleases. What the Rulers do to their subjects or the citizens will follow them. Corruption, injustice, oppression, pride, adamance, ruthlessness, murder, avarice, and their associate practices are abominations in the sight of God. For them to rise above political culture, they should aim at execution of justice and righteousness while in the service of God, where the vertical and horizontal relationships should be upheld towards God and fellow people respectively. No lip service in worshipping God is acceptable in the sight of God because He sees everything. He knows our intentions and deeds done in secret or public. To be wise rulers, run away from sin and the wrath of God and be truly penitent before death strikes for there is no repentance after death. To do so, is to rise above culture that is involved in sinful acts that raise the anger of God.

The role of the church is needed

It seems sins are rapidly multiplying in the world which might imply that more people are conforming to the world rather than being transformed. Are these the signs of the end of the known time to happen just before the Parousia as alluded to in MATTHEW 24:4–14 and 2 TIMOTHY 3:1–9? Whatever these evil practices signify, they need to be fought against by the governments and the church for people to be liberated from the prevalent life-threatening situations in the world. They cause havoc, anarchy, restlessness, ailments, immorality, economic retrogression and unnecessary suffering and deaths in the society.

The church must effectively play its role of teaching the youngsters and the adults to adopt the correct attitudes that will produce good behaviour and character in individuals. The church is the divine institution for spiritual and moral liberation. The liberated believers will adhere to the Christian norms and values as the standard of living in the community or society, violation of which calls for disciplinary action. A person has the right to live but reckless living should not be viewed as a right. Permissive living should not be tolerated because it fans fire of insubordination and moral decadence which will retard social, moral and economic development. The church uses the persuasive approach of winning the souls of the people which might not be very effective to arrogant people. The government, on the other hand can use the law enforcement agents to control mischief of the arrogant subjects or citizens. Disciplinary actions should be effected by the government.

Parents and schools should work hand in glove to give some informal and formal moral education. Some adults should cease to deliberately indoctrinate children with teachings of violence in the society which make them behave wildly. How can responsible people delight in violence when we claim to be civilised or Christians who fear God? The people who are supportive of immoral acts while they claim to be Christians are in essence pseudo–Christians who need to repent to be forgiven by God. Anything evil should not be supported for it is an abomination to God who is holy.

Church denominations should unite as the United army of the cross to fight against any evil activity that dehumanises innocent people for their owner is none other than God, the Sovereign Ruler. Prevalent malpractices nowadays in the societies are, totalitarianism, war, robbery, debauchery, corruption, bribery, profiteering, nepotism, human trafficking, marriage breakdowns, child abuse, social instability owing to lack of employment, poverty, low standards of education, deteriorating health standards, owing to negligence and hate politics. Can the universal church's voice be heard to alert the world to unite to fight against these social problems to liberate people from bondage? Can the church be the voice of the voiceless to bring about sanity and peace in the world? When the church keeps quiet that means it is supporting the status quo. Are we, as the church, not our brothers' and sisters' keepers? To rise above culture needs courage, endurance, patience, sacrifice and commitment to effect changes for the better in the lives of the people.

Jesus, in His sermon on the mount said, *"Blessed are the peacemakers for they shall be called children of God"* (**Matthew 5:9**). What Jesus calls good and who Jesus says blessed can be seen to be contrary to earthly point of views and upside down. Preaching the word of God in some parts of the world is wrong and prohibited, yet it is meant to put things the right side up. This happened to the Christian believers in the early church when they were accused of preaching the word of God. The accusers said, *"These who have turned the world upside down have come here too. Jason has harboured them and these are all acting contrary to the decrees of Caesar, saying there is another king– Jesus"* (**Acts 17:6–7**). Let us, as the church, take the lead in solving the social problems of the world where we spot them to be so prevalent. Our Lord Jesus said to His followers, *"You are the salt of the earth. But if the salt loses its saltness, how can it be made salty again? It is no longer good for anything, except to be thrown out and trampled underfoot"* (**Matthew 5:13**). Jesus also said, *"You are the light of the world. A town built on a hill cannot be hidden"* (**Matthew 5:14**). "Sal terrae et lux mundi,"- *"salt of the earth and the light of the world"*, is so appealing to be a suitable motto of a transforming church in the world for people to rise above a culture that is debilitating, through God's help. Hallelujah!

REFERENCES

1. NIV Study Bible
2. King James Bible
3. Oxford Compact English Dictionary second edition revised
4. The United Methodist Church Book of Discipline 2012
5. www.churchofjesuschrist.org on Isaiah **40:31**
6. Peake's Commentary

www.ingramcontent.com/pod-product-compliance
Lightning Source LLC
Chambersburg PA
CBHW042116100526
44587CB00025B/4072